I WROTE THIS FOR YOU

just the words

IAIN S. THOMAS

central
avenue
publishing
2013

Dedication

Thank you.
Thank you for finding me.
Thank you for being here.
I've waited for you longer than the stars
have waited for the night.
Since time started ticking.
Without you reading them, these words mean nothing.
Thank you for giving them meaning.
There are many different ways to read this book.
You can read it from start to finish.
You can skip to a part of it that resonates
with where you are right now.
You can leave it next to your bed or in the bottom of a backpack
and every now and again, pull it out and randomly pick a page.
More often than not, I have found that the universe will help
you pick the right page.
You can circle something and hand it to someone else. This can
be quite powerful but in the end, remember: This is your book.
Read it how you want to.

I wrote this for you.

Thank you for reading it.

ON LOVE FOUND.

ON BEING IN LOVE.

ON LOVE LOST.

ON DESPAIR.

ON HOPE.

ON LIVING.

ON DYING.

ON LOVE FOUND.

The Strangest Books

You've written my story backwards. You've taken my chapter out your book. Now I'm just a prologue. A dedication.

For you.

The First Sign Is Taking Strange Pictures

I have pretended to go mad in order to tell you the things I need to. I call it art.

Because art is the word we give to our feelings made public. And art doesn't worry anyone.

The Light Of Future Memories

You make me nostalgic for a love that hasn't even happened yet.

The Lipstick On The Window

The words "I love you" become nothing but noise. But that's why we kiss. To say with our lips what we couldn't before.

The Shape Of Air

You love the way air moves. And now I can no longer breathe.

The Day Tomorrow Came

I know you're busy doing all the things you always planned to do but remember, today is also the day that you kiss me.

The Loneliest Personal Ad

Introvert seeks someone you can't trust. Apply without.

The Seat Next To You

When I sit near you, my hands suddenly become alien things and I don't know where to put them or what they usually do, like this is the first time I've ever had hands and maybe they go in my pockets and maybe they don't.

The Shipwreck In My Head

Everything you do, you pay for. So if you're going to kiss me, you'd best be prepared to bleed.

The Amazing Something

The feeling you get when you think of something amazing then forget it and know that it felt amazing but you can't remember the details. Then, minutes later, you remember it again and you're so grateful because you nearly lost something amazing, forever. Except, this time, it's a person. Not an idea.

The Bleach

You are your hair and your eyes and your thoughts. You are what you look at and what you feel and what you do about it. The light from the sun is still a part of the sun. My thoughts of you are as real as any part of you.

The Missed Appointment

So yes, we could kiss. I could kiss you and you could kiss me. There's no science, plane ticket or clock stopping us. But if we kiss, it will end the world. And I've ended the world before. No one survived. Least of all me.

The Shape Falls At Your Feet

Maybe it's because you're one of those people who believes that sometimes, the most reckless thing you can do with your heart, is not being reckless with it.

The Clearly Labeled

I think you'll find you're mistaken. My name is clearly written across
the front and I recognise the scratch down the side (that happened in
high school). This is my heart.
You can't just come here, and take it.

The Send/Delete

I've written you a hundred messages that I'll never send.

The Blown Away

I am far more delicate than you can possibly imagine.
You need to move slowly.

The Train Of Lies

I say that I won't touch you.

But my fingers are liars.

I tell you how I won't hold you.

But my arms are going to hell.

I promise I won't kiss you.

But my lips break it.

I let you know that I won't love you.

But my heart has no conscience.

And no part of me will apologise.

The Drive Before Dawn

I read what you leave in public spaces. The songs you reference. The quotes you quote. I know it's about me. I can feel you thinking of me. I want to tell you that I know and admit that I feel the same. But I can't. Not yet.

The Listening

I want to listen to you. I want to open the door. I want you to tell me your story, in your words. The books don't do it justice.
I can't hear you unless you speak.

The Never Ending Search For Something Real

I spend most of my nights outside, looking for ways to make you smile.

The Corner Of Me & You

I don't know if you felt that or not.

But it felt like two people kissing after hours of thinking about it.

It felt like two people talking after nights of silence.

It felt like two people touching after weeks of being numb.

It felt like two people facing each other after months of looking away.

It felt like two people in love after years of being alone.

And it felt like two people meeting each other, after an entire lifetime of not meeting each other.

The Songs We Sing

Somewhere, someone knows the words to the songs you sing.

The Walking Away

There are days when I want to walk up to you and scream in your face "No one else gets you like I do, now let's get the hell out of here."

The Lantern In The Lifeboat

I am nervous. I'm afraid. But I will stand here in the white hot heat of you. I will play Russian roulette with your playlists. I will tell jokes I'm not sure you'll find funny. I will hold on until there is no more reason to.
And in the end, I will break the stars and resurrect the sun.

The Far From Home

I would find you down the line with broken wings, pick you up, and swear that you would taste the sky again.

The New Colour

And their shape and their hair and their eyes and their smell and their voice. That suddenly, these things can exist and you're not quite sure how they existed without you knowing about them before.

The Closer

You lie in bed, staring at the ceiling and counting crows.

Someone.

Anyone.

But anyone could be someone if only you looked a little closer.

The Circle, Triangle, Square

If you've got the time, we can play a game. It's easy. We just see if I'm the same shape as the space you have inside you. If everything fits, we both win. If it doesn't, don't force it. That's how you get splinters in your heart.

The Excuse For Your Company

I was wondering if you had a second. To talk about anything at all.

The Point Of Contact

And then my soul saw you and it kind of went
"Oh there you are. I've been looking for you."

The Wet Hair And Eyes

You are a drop of perfect in an imperfect world.
And all I need, is a taste.

The Ghost Train

And if you can't say yes, answer anyway. Because I'd rather live with
the answer than die with the question.

The Sleep

You dreamed me one night. Now I'm dreaming you back.

The Reminders In The Sky

You are the distance between the way things are and the way I want
them to be.

The Shape Of It

They want me. I want you. And you want someone else.
But none of us want to turn around.

The Pattern Is A System Is A Maze

Of course it's complicated. If it wasn't, I probably wouldn't be interested in you.

The Reflection

You told me that there were two of me, in me. The me I pretended to be. And the real me.
You asked me to guess which one you loved more.

You kissed me before I could answer and in that moment, I knew.

The Way Saturn Turns

All I can do, if I feel this way, is trust that somewhere in the universe, there's a you that feels the same.

The Skyscrapers Meet By The Side Of The Road

We look at the people who tell the truth, who say real things in public, like they're confused. Crazy.

As if everything should be said safely or not at all and what you feel shouldn't be taken seriously.

Which is why it's not polite to say
"I'm going to kiss you now because I can't do anything else."

The Wasted Words

You will forgive me, I hope you don't mind me saying, I just wanted to add, if you've got time and I've said it before and I'll say it again, because you should know, before we go any further, we should put everything on the table because the reality is and the truth is and the fact of the matter is, I shouldn't interrupt but I was wondering and if you know, please tell me, how we manage to say so much, without saying anything at all.

The Building We Could Burn

I burnt my tongue on you. Now I've lost all sense of taste. Or decency.

The Tallness Of Things

Falling buildings matter less than you noticing me. Because the world is big. And here, next to you, I am small.

The Place Before Now

My stranger on a train. I make up stories about you as we click-clack across the city, pulses of blood along veins of industry and commerce. One huge beating, pumping city and you and I are single celled. Red blood going in. Blue blood coming out at 5:30pm. How was your day? Do you enjoy what you do? Do you pretend to enjoy what you do? Who do you love? Do they kiss the sweat from your forehead? Do they whisper in your ear? How do you take your coffee?

This is my stop. I'll see you tomorrow.

The Tender Tinder Box

You've made the air flammable. These walls are just paper. And blood is gasoline. You shouldn't have come here, made of fireworks, if you didn't want me to play with fire. I need a light.

The Stars

I pass you every day. Our eyes meet every now and again and we nod our mutually agreeable greeting. Safely.

I'd rather sweep you off your feet. Say something. Anything. To you. Take you to the top of my building and show you the stars. Dance in the moonlight. A glass of wine.

Maybe tomorrow.

The Sparks In The Ceiling

The sky was made so clear that sometimes, at night, you can see the far blue edge of forever behind distant suns. Yet, nothing's that clear here, and I'm sitting right next to you.

The Moths Don't Die For Nothing

I'm sure people just kiss each other. I'm sure that sometimes you're talking and somehow two people move closer and closer to each other and then, they just kiss. I'm sure it happens all the time. But I'm also sure that a kiss is never just a kiss.

The Brace Position

I'll tell you the truth so close to your lips it'll taste like a lie. There's a tongue in my mouth. It matters. This fucking matters.

The only thing that works is the truth and you are the hardest truth to tell.

So kiss like you give a damn.

The Art Of Otherness

I could never tell you because then you'd hear nothing but words. I had to wait until you could feel it yourself.

The Longest Distance

It would be easier if reaching out to you, didn't mean reaching in.

The Petals Fall Through Time

This time, the time machine took me back to the right place.

This time, I ran outside and nearly grabbed myself before I walked out that door to kiss you for the first time.

But this time, another me stopped me, before I could stop me, and said

"The only thing worse than missing someone, is wondering what there was to miss."

This time, I sat down with me, and we drank and we spoke about how different things could've been. For me. And for me.

Later, I still kissed you for the first time. This time.

The Feeling Of Someone Drawing You

And if you want to know the feeling I'm talking about, run your own fingers slowly through your hair, and pretend they're someone else's.

The Burning Compass

My atoms and chemicals could've been made anywhere in the universe, but they were made here, near you. Near yours.

The Rules Of Engagement

All persons entering a heart do so at their own risk. Management can and will be held responsible for any loss, love, theft, ambition or personal injury. Please take care of your belongings. Please take care of the way you look at me. No roller skating, kissing, smoking, fingers through hair, 3am phone calls, stained letters, littering, unfeeling feelings, a smell left on a pillow, doors slammed, lyrics whispered, or loitering. Thank you.

The Static

I know how you felt about me. I knew all along. You'd break up a little, become a little more static, whenever you spoke to me and you were always trying to figure out ways to be near me. It was obvious. I'm sorry I didn't return your feelings, I was an idiot and a fool. And it's got nothing to do with who you become, seriously, I'm really sorry. Please, give me a call sometime.

The Fragile Arc

It may have just been a moment to you, but it changed every single one that followed for me.

ON BEING IN LOVE.

The Carrington Event

Love proudly. Let it burn anything between you.

The Whisper Waits

I have met so many people in my life that have made me fall in love. But you, you are the first that has made me stay in love. And I will be with you forever.

The Purpose Of Love

When I don't know how I'm supposed to feel, you're the only person that can remind me.

The Voice In The Back Of My Heart

When you have nothing left to say to me, say it anyway.

The Forest Of Stars

There's no point in me saying I miss you
(I miss you).

The Remaining Me

Even after the entire world has taken me apart, there's still a part of me left for you.

The Desire To Live Underwater Forever

If I breathe you in and you breathe me out, I swear we can breathe forever. I swear I'll find summer in your winter and spring in your autumn and always, hands at the ends of your fingers, arms at the ends of your shoulders and I swear, when we run out of forever, when we run out of air, your name will be the last word that my lungs make air for.

The Books Never Written

Dragons, angels, gnomes, creatures beneath the earth that make words with hammers, a shooting star that shoots back, rain falling from the ground to the sky, bars that refuse to serve dwarfs or wanderers, a fountain that makes you young (and lonely) while those around you grow old, saplings that know everything, a sea made of tears from every lover who never loved, a silver boat with a sail made of pages from all the books that were never written.

All my dreams are beautiful. But none as beautiful as you. You are the reason I return here each morning.

The Last Land I Stood On

And my fingers are ships sailing on your skin, slowly drifting and hoping against hope that they fall off the edge of the earth.

And your heart is nothing but the gravity pulling me towards you.

The Time Keeps Twisting Me

The seconds take a part of me with them. Hopefully to you.

The Language Stripped Naked

And I'm sorry I ever learned any words that make you cry.

I'm still doing my best to learn the ones that make you smile.

The Forgotten Feeling

I know there was something before you.

I just can't remember what it was.

The Tick-Tock In Your Chest

I will hold you so tightly and carefully when I see you again.

Like crystal. Or an atom bomb.

The Zodiac Of One

When I look up at night, all the constellations look like you.

The Wishing Well In The Sky (Letters To Father Time)

All I ask is that you let me spend forever feeling this way, before you take me.

The Things Which Aren't Love

Your salary is not love and your word is not love. Your clothes are not love and holding hands is not love. Sex is not love and a kiss is not love. Long letters are not love and a text is not love. Flowers are not love and a box of chocolates is not love. Sunsets are not love and photographs are not love. The stars are not love and a beach under the moonlight is not love. The smell of someone else on your pillow is not love and the feeling of their skin touching your skin is not love. Heart-shaped candy is not love and an overseas holiday is not love. The truth is not love and winning an argument is not love. Warm coffee isn't love and cheap cards bought from stores are not love. Tears are not love and laughter is not love. A head on a shoulder is not love and messages written at the front of books given as gifts are not love. Apathy is not love and numbness is not love. A pain in your chest is not love and clenching your fist is not love. Rain is not love.

Only you. Only you, are love.

The Absence Of Oxygen

Forget the air. I'll breathe you instead.

The Last Place We Saw Them

Gasping for air and sanity. Moon and stars and clouds and night. Out of breath and breathless. Pillows and sheets and blankets and you. I will drown in this bed. They say it's just like going to sleep.

The Endless Punchline

Great, real, true love should feel like an inside joke that only you and them can laugh at. No matter what the world does to either of you.

The Waves Put You To Sleep

I love you like I love the sea. And I'm ok with drowning.

The Place Where I Wait

I'll see you at your funeral, if you'll see me at mine. I'll wait at the edges for your ghost to rise (until the end of time). We'll find someplace nice to haunt, an abandoned beach house filled with memories of summer sunburns. Children will giggle as we tickle their feet at night and they'll never know the bad dreams we fight. We'll make our own heaven. Walking in places we used to walk until death, dies.

The Heart Beats Per Minute

You are the best parts of all the songs I love.

The Slight Pinch

You and I could collide, like atoms in some scientist's wet dream. We could start a new universe together. We could mix like a disease. And if we do, I hope we never get better.

The Lovers Bleed Into Each Other

And as we touch, I can never tell if you are touching me or I am touching you.

The Afternoon

And I would kiss the sweat from your brow.

And you would let me.

The Things That Are Left

The world made me cold. You made me water.

One day we'll be clouds.

The Needle And Ink

Look at you, like a new tattoo. Because I might not always have you but I'll have the feeling of you for the rest of my life.

The View From Our Kingdom

Get the bedding and the pillows. Get a mattress too (we'll need all the sheets in the house). We're going to build a fort.
And it's only going to be big enough, for just me and you.

The Static On The Line

Don't talk to me like you know me. Talk to me like you love me.

The Circus Is Cheaper When It Rains

I've taken the same ride too many times.

I could fall asleep in the loop.

I know the clowns wipe the fake, makeup smiles off their faces once the show is done.

I know the lions sleep in cages at night.

I know the tightrope walkers have blisters on their feet.

I know the ringmaster doesn't believe in what he yells to the crowd anymore.

I know the strongman, isn't as strong as he once was.

I know the candy floss has always been, just sugar and air.

You are the only reason I come back here every night.

The Untouchable City

That's what it feels like when you touch me. Like millions of tiny universes being born and then dying in the space between your finger and my skin. Sometimes I forget.

The Promise Sleep Made Me

Every bed without you in it, is broken.

The Song Across The Wires

I'm a picture without a frame.
A poem without a rhyme.
A car with three wheels.
A sun without fire.
I am a gun without bullets.
I am the truth without someone to hear it.
I am a feeling without someone to feel it.
This is who I am.
A mess without you.
Something beautiful with you.

The Things We Could Do Today

Let's pretend we're artists and everything we feel is something new to be proud of. Let's take our imaginary friends on a double date and ditch them in a movie and hope they get along while we kiss outside on the sidewalk. Let's take the dreams you mumbled in your sleep and paint a child's nursery. And if we don't finish today, we've always got tomorrow.

The Light We Fly To

Which is why you make me feel like a moth that's reached the moon.

The Place Where Nothing Hurts

There is no music, just the sound of the wind and the leaves it touches. But hopefully that'll be music enough, for you.

The Well Of Dreams

To wake up next to you. And confirm that the images I saw on the back of my eyelids seconds before, have all been made real.

The Heart Rides On

I love you. I love your eyes. I love your smell. I love your hair. I love your laugh. I love your skin. I love everything inside you. And I'll try to make all the parts that I find, happy.

Because you make me happy. So much.

The Fire At Sea

When the tide goes out for the last time, all the shipwrecks will be waiting for us and the bones of the earth will shine bright white in the sun.

When the tide goes out for the last time, I'll meet you by the planes that never made it past Bermuda.

When the tide goes out for the last time, I swear, we will have nothing left to lose.

The Space Between

You are the silence between the notes. The white space between the letters. The missing that makes everything else, a something.

The Tired Advice

But love is none of these things. It won't suddenly make every day ok. It won't change who you are. It won't make your car go faster. It doesn't even wash your dishes.

All love is, is love. And that's all it needs to be, really.

The Long Time Coming

I never stopped loving you. Because I never stopped breathing.

The Talk

The conversation between your fingers and someone else's skin. This is the most important discussion you can ever have.

The Ugly

We were both so ugly inside. But we made each other beautiful.

The Jewels

Nature crowned you with dew as you lay there sleeping. Like a web after the rain. Like stars in the night sky. I didn't want to wake you. I just wanted to sit and watch a while longer.

The First Sip

I always wanted you. Even when I had you. I could drink from you forever and never be any less thirsty than I was that first day. The day I realised how parched I'd always been.

The New Species

I want to weave you into me. Stick your thorns in and grow. Bleed sap and feel this shining light. Grow strange leaves. Bear this fruit. Share this soil. Bury ourselves. Reach for the sun. Strip this bark. Carve a name and a heart into me. Please.

The AWOL Hearts

Let's play hopscotch in malls. Let's drive fast with the top down. Let's turn up the music as loud as it'll go. Let's put a couch on an island in the middle of the freeway and wave at everyone on their way to work. Let's hug strangers in parking lots. Let's hand out secret messages at traffic lights. Let's make lists of all the things that make us smile and tick them off, one at a time. The world will carry on without you and me when we're gone.

Let it carry on without us, today.

The Room Is Nearly Empty

I already know what your plans for the weekend are.

I've been thoroughly briefed on the weather.

I've extrapolated your metaphors to illustrate your point.

I've heard your dissertation on what's wrong with the world.

I've paraded along next to your monologue.

So please. For me.

Fill this silence with the words you promised to say.

The Only Part Of You I Love

You could ink yourself until everyone knows all the things you love. You could wear uniforms that gave you all the authority in the world. Lose weight until there was nothing left. Paint the face. Suck in your gut.

But in the dark, stripped down to your bones, all that remains is you.

The Humans Aren't Recyclable

I hold you like I do, tightly because I know that one day, I'll die.

And I am determined to do it with a smile on my face.

The Fury Of Water

You can try and hold me back. Build your damn walls, pack sandbags along the edges and yell at the clouds and the rain and the sky to stop.

But I will not relent. I will reach you. Because I am the sea. And I will continue to love you no matter what.

The First Crack Is The Last

I lied when I told you I forgot. I know it doesn't seem like a big thing but I wanted to tell you the truth and never, ever lie to you.

Because that's how it starts.

The Hidden Depths

You've got to keep looking for them, even after you find them. Otherwise, you lose them.

The Sound Of The Sea

May I see the things in front of me as they are, not as I think them to be.

May I walk the steps ahead of me one at a time, not wondering if there's a map.

May I say the things that fix things, not break them further apart.

May I do what I need to do, not be distracted by what I can't.

May I dream of what I hope for, not of what I fear.

May I love you like I love you, not as any other, me.

The Ticket Is Valid

And maybe I'll sleep at the station because there's nothing to go home to but an empty fridge and some stale mayonnaise.

And maybe I'll make friends with the guys sleeping under cardboard boxes and newspapers and we'll discuss what it means to love and to live.

And maybe I'll wander the city, one lost particle in a dust storm of Mondays, late nights and reports due yesterday.

And maybe I'll get on a plane or a ship and get lost in places I've never been lost in before.

And maybe I'll keep my phone on me in case you call. And tell me there's something to come home to.

The First Time We Met

It's when you hold eye contact for that second too long or maybe the way you laugh. It sets off a flash and our memories take a picture of who we are at that point when we first know

"This is love."

And we clutch that picture to our hearts because we expect each other to always be the people in that picture. But people change. People aren't pictures. And you can either take a new picture or throw the old one away.

The Burning

You were tired and weary, your eyes heavy. I'd have given anything to be able to just pick you up and carry you home. I'd have run the whole way. But I couldn't.
The sun is up and you're still there, finishing what you started. My arms will be ready.

The To Not Do List

There are a million important things to do. But none as important as lying here next to you.

The Peace In The Disturbance

I'll do every dish ever made. I'll change as much as I can without changing who I am. Just promise me you'll stay.

The Glitter Phoenix Burns Again

I won't compose prose every morning you open your eyes next to me (I won't compare you to a summer's day).

I won't kiss the tears from your cheeks whenever you cry.

I won't remember every appointment.

I won't keep the sheen on my armour.

I won't know what to say sometimes.

I won't get your order right.

I'll be late.

I'll fuck up.

But I'll write something for you when you least expect it (in summer or winter).

But I'll hold you as tight as I can whenever I can.

But I'll burst through the door as soon as I remember.

But I'll polish it until it shines again.

But I'll say something anyway.

But I'll go back and make it right.

But I'll get there.

But I'll try.

The Relative Phenomena

I would do my taxes. Fill out insurance forms.

Count grains of rice in a bag.

Whatever made time pass the slowest with you.

The Beautiful Mess We Could Be

So may you find in each other what you came here for. And trust that this is love because it is (love is trust). And tangled lives you may lead but into each other, never apart, till you cannot distinguish between being and being together.

The Shot Stars

If your star falls down, you will find mine lying beside yours.

The Air In My Lungs

When sadness was the sea, you were the one that taught me to swim.

The Secret Place

I wish I could keep you in the box I keep things in that I never want to lose.

The Divine Mechanic

Never give up on anything you haven't done absolutely everything to save. Even if what you're saving, kills you.

The Avoidance Of Pain

I would never hurt you. Not even to kiss it better.

The Fear Of Air

Maybe I come from dust. And maybe the air and the lights and the world will one day tear me apart and to dust, I will return. But if you ever see me again, in this life or the next, there will be enough of me left, to become a rock.

Or something, at least, that you can lean on.

The Envy Of A Billion Little Unique Snowflakes

I don't care what people think. I fell in love with you. Not people.

The Metal Starts To Twist

I'm lost and looking for the sky, for moving parts and a place that doesn't rust. For wheels that burn and a world that turns. For a road that phantom cars still drive down while lovers long lost feel wind that's blown too long in silver hair.

You are the only map I know.

The Time It Takes To Fall

So if all we have is that glance in the window. If all we have is till this train stops. If all we have is till the sun comes up, till your lift picks you up. And if all we have is till the day I die. I'm ok with what we have.

The Commerce

I would set up shop inside your heart and charge the world to love you.

The Water

You make me want to drink water. Not soda. A salad. Run every morning. Get enough sleep. So when I end, I'll know I had all the time I could get, with you.

The Picture We Make

Fine. Maybe I'm the puzzle. But you're still the pieces.

The Onion Of Us

You want me to be made of the same thin paper as you. But it'd feel like I was kissing cardboard.

The Inscription

This is how I live. This is how I live. This is how I live.

I mumble things under my breath, three times so I'll remember.

This where I live. This is where I live. This is where I live.

Inside the sun, beneath the burning trees.

This is how I love. This is how I love. This is how I love.

Touching you, in case there comes a time I can't.

This is where I love. This is where I love. This is where I love.

In the heart of things, on the tips of waves.

This is how I die. This is how I die. This is how I die.

Too fast, not long enough.

This where I die. This is where I die. This is where I die.

Here.

The Place We Were In

And strum my fingers gently across your skin, like I was playing the slowest love song in the world and only you and I could hear it.

The Station

Fuck it. You throw a dart at a map, we'll go there and start new. Somewhere else in the world that's not here. Somewhere where we haven't said things to each other that we can't unsay and done things which we can't undo.

There we can say new things. We can do new things. And those new things we say and do will be more important than the old things. Let's leave. Please. Leave with me.

The Scars You Love

There are a million ways to bleed.

But you are by far my favourite.

The Storm Before The Calm

You're still here but I am still the sea. And as peaceful as I seem, please don't ever turn your back on me.

ON LOVE LOST.

The Last Night

That last night we spent together, when we both knew it was over, and you called me that name that only you had for me, that sound more than a name that you'd never say in front of anyone else; I'm sorry I turned away and cried and asked you why you called me that. I didn't mean ever, I didn't mean I'd always hated the name, I meant that name meant so much to me, but I knew soon no one would ever call me that again and it hurt more than I could bear.

The Dirt Beneath Fingernails

Even though cold is colder. Far is further. Now is longer. Even though it takes so long to dig myself out of you. I still dig.

The Colours Of Stolen Sleep

Now I'm awake and you're here.
Now I'm dreaming and you're here.
Now I have nothing but days.

Never nights.

The Echo Inspector

"Why am I still here?"

"You're not. You're a ghost."

"I thought I left."

"You did. You're always leaving."

"Where am I now?"

"Always here. Never here again."

The Stillness Of Patience

When you can, let me know how long you're willing to miss me for.

The Salting Of The Earth

You should know that there is something worse than hate and that is unlove.

Because hate is anger over something lost, hate is passion, hate is misguided, it's caring for the wrong things but it is still caring.

But unlove, unlove is to unkiss, to unremember, to unhold, to undream, to undo everything that ever was and leave smooth stone behind in its wake.

No fire.

No fury.

Just, nothing.

And that is worse than hate.

The Chameleons Live In The City

I guess you're proud of yourself for not trying to change me, even though all I ever wanted to do, was change.

The Point Past Peak Feelings

I know you have feelings left somewhere. But they're all so hard to reach.

The Invisible Postal Service

I keep thinking you already know. I keep thinking I've sent you letters that were only ever written in my mind.

The Dearly Discarded

Late at night, when your brain is tired of thinking of everything else, you will find me there. You cannot throw me far enough away.

The Night Is A Tunnel

I have told the sky all my loneliest thoughts of you. And all it does is shine starlight back at me. But I guess that's what makes it such a good listener.

The Fading Glow

What you gave me was a reason. Not an excuse. Because there's sex, making love and fucking. And then there's you.

The Empty Classroom

You taught me how to be alone.
And I learned my lesson, in your absence.

The Skeletons In The Sea

Truth is the last thing I can take because it's the last thing you took.

The Seraphim And The Pirate

You were better to the ones that were worse for you. And worse to the one that was better for you.

The Stranger In You

My parents gave me a book and it told me I was made of dirt and dust. But you, you were made of ash.

The Ebb And Flow

I know I'm only borrowing it. I know I have to give Summer back to you. Just as you, have to give Winter, back to me.

The Bastards Tied Me Down

You may continue to call it a breakup.

I will continue to call it an exorcism.

The Truth Is Ugly

In the movies, the person leaving you never has a blocked nose when they cry. And all their tears are pretty.

The Floor Takes So Long To Hit

Congratulations. You took me down. And now, you have made everything that is sad, relevant.

The Shade

You were always my dark cloud that let me stare at the sun.

The End Of That

If you thought that was our second chance, you're wrong. It was
our last.

The History Of Arson

When you lived here, it was a city.

When you left, it became a town.

The Things Sold By The Sea Shore

I could've sworn I was telling the truth when I told you I didn't
miss you.

The Tales From The Bar

You're just another story I can't tell anymore.

The World Is Too Big

All the space without you in it, is empty.

The Error Of Parallax

The only reason I hate you now is because I loved you then.

The Tiny Iceberg

The little things you forget, kill me.

The Sea Reclaims The Land

I know you're just a rag doll now, sewn together with memories that we might have had.

I know you're just the dream inside of a dream

And don't worry, I know I don't know you, anymore.

The Simple Shattering Of Water

It's because you and them were made of the same pieces. And afterwards, when you put yourself back together, some piece of them remained.

The Leave Behind

I don't know who you're kissing now. But I do know who you think about when you do.

The B Train

I'd leave the memory of you at the station, if it didn't already know the way home.

The Cupboard Is Empty

I'm all out of midnight phone calls and flowers sent to your door. I'm out of throwing letters off fire escapes and drawing a cathedral in the sand. I'm out of spray-painting your name on freeway overpasses. I'm low on cute names given between blankets and 9am. I've got no dramatic displays of public affection left. And now everyone else I ever love is going to think me boring. Because I used it all up on you.

The Stranger In Waiting

I'm sure you've met them. They say they'll put you back together while they're tearing everything apart. And they use the type of lips you can taste for years.

The Paint Hides The Brick

You took all my words when all I wanted to do was say them.

The Diaries Of Foreign Lovers

You are so patriotic to your heart. It keeps the country together. But it tears the world apart.

The Whispering At The Back

You say the things you don't need to say.

Because it hurts when you don't say them.

The Art Of Breathing

And in the beginning, my lungs had too much air in them, whenever you were near, like I could never breathe out enough.

And in the end, my throat closed, whenever you were far, like I could never breathe in again.

The Speed Of Feeling

Now you've gone too fast. Now, you've made me leave me behind.

The Act Of Normalcy

I hope they make you happy. That's what I'll say.

The Ghost Ships

I won't keep circling the ocean forever, hoping I'll spot your island on the horizon, uncolonised and flying an old, tattered flag. You on the shore with the sand between your toes.

The Grim Alternatives

I love no one but you, I have discovered, but you are far away and I am here alone. Then this is my life and maybe, however unlikely, I'll find my way back there. Or maybe, one day, I'll settle for second best. And on that same day, hell will freeze over, the sun will burn out and the stars will fall from the sky.

The One I Miss

Just say goodbye. You can say it when you get up from the couch. You can say it at the door. I will say it when you get to your car. I'll scream it as you drive away.

The Goodbye Song

So if you can't stay, walk away slowly. Rip the plaster off bit by bit, piece by piece. Because I'd rather feel that than nothing at all.

The Space Left

I miss you sitting next to me. I miss you falling asleep. I miss carrying you to bed. I miss looking at the ceiling and listening to you breathing.

I miss you. I miss you. I miss you.

The Big Blue Sea

I don't care how many fish there are in the sea. I don't want a fish. I want you.

The More Than Three

Wish you were here. Wish I was there. Wish it was different. Wish wishes came true.

I'd wish you back.

The Distraction Of Time

So I sat there on the bench and got lost in the faces of people I'd never know or meet because like them, my life is too busy for strangers.

I missed the train today. And you.

The Twins

I like to think that somewhere out there, on a planet exactly like ours, two people exactly like you and me made totally different choices and that, somewhere, we're still together.

That's enough for me.

The Dark Room

In this room. With the curtains drawn. With the lights on.

The sun shining outside. This is where you hurt the most.

The Missing Machine

There's a folder of pictures I can't open.
There's so many songs that don't sound the same.
There's a number I can't dial and a message I can't send.
There's a restaurant I can't eat at, not with any friends.
There's words and names I can only say in my head.
There's a pair of eyes that belong to you, that I can never look into again.

The Air I Saved For Later

You say that the way I feel, it's all just chemicals in my brain.

It's all just strange air in my atmosphere.

It's all just new colours in my rivers.

But you are my industry.

You are my factory.

You are my smoke stacks.

You are my production line.

You are my cheap sneakers.

You are my fast food.

And I'm a planet you once called home.

That's nearly out of air.

The Strangers Were Lovers

You look at me, now, like this and think
"This is who they were all along."

But this is just who I am to other people.
And you became other people.

The Age At Which It Happens

One day, you realise that there are some people you'll never see again.
At least, not in the same way.

The Mechanics Of Puppetry

I guess I should say thank you, for cutting all my strings. But if it's all the same to you, I wish you'd left my wings.

The Water Is On Fire

I'm not scared of never meeting you. I'm scared of having met you, and let you go.

The Blue Lines

I couldn't convince you that the blue you see is the same blue that I see. But maybe that's how lovers know they're meant to love; they see the same blue. And they both know it.

The Monsters I Miss

And every single thing you ever did that bothered me, is every single thing I miss.

The Scratches That Made Me

You buy things and you keep them clean. You take care of them. Keep them in a special pocket. Away from keys and coins. Away from other things that should be kept clean and taken care of as well. Then they get scratched. And scratched again. And again. And again. And again. Soon, you don't care about them anymore. You don't keep them in a special pocket. You throw them in the bag with everything else. They've surpassed their form and become nothing but function. People are like that. You meet them and keep them clean. In a special pocket. And then you start to scratch them. Not on purpose. Sometimes you just drop them by accident or forget which pocket they're in. But after the first scratch, it's all downhill from there. You see past their form. They become function. They are a purpose. Only their essence remains.

The Heart Is Red

I'm sorry. But you could never tell the difference between the mood you were in, and me.

The Fade To Nothing

As you drift further into the past, my memory of you fractures and splinters until all I can clearly remember is not a picture but a feeling.

The Clarification

I remember more the time we spent driving nowhere than the fancy dinner.

I remember more the time we spent laughing and drawing than when we stepped on stage.

I remember more the silence in each others arms than the conversations about how we felt.

I remember more of what I didn't expect to remember with you.

The Bibliography Of Strings

And you taught me what this feels like.

And then how it feels to lose it.

And you showed me who I wanted.

And then who I wasn't.

And you ticked every box.

And then drew a line.

And you weren't mine to begin with.

And then not to end with.

And you looked like everything I wanted.

And then became something I hated.

And you get thought of every day.

And then not in a good way.

And you let me leave.

And then wish I'd stayed.

And you almost killed me.

But I didn't die.

The Rose Is Not Always A Rose

You can be in love and you can be in a relationship. But they're not always the same thing.

The Pain Unfelt

I have told myself you are not allowed to hurt me anymore. That's what hurts the most.

The One And Nothing

One.

Two words.

Then three words.

The fourth is "love".

The fifth word is "you".

Six say: "I love you", twice.

I can't begin to comprehend seven words.

Eight is far, you and I are closer.

In nine words' time, we'll be reaching the conclusion.

And ten — which is just one, nothing and the end.

The Nothing

When love begins, it's easy for you to make something out of nothing.

When it ends, it's much harder to turn that something back
into nothing.

The Red

When hurt turns red and a piece of your heart is missing. When the
cold bites deep and you've got that feeling like you just got out of
surgery. When the only way to stay sane is to concentrate on anything
else but how you feel. When you count the tiles in the ceiling. When
you push the earphones closer. When the first day of winter arrives.
When you remember every nuance of every word of every time. When
all this happens.

Embrace it. Feel every feeling. Cry every tear. Sob every sob. Because
this is what it feels like to have loved.

The Way It Rains Down Windows

And there are thousands in the crowd outside every day. And
everyone's there. And they love me. And I don't care. Because they're
not you.

The Things I Say Before I Go

I pray you're ok. That it's ok. I pray all the parts of you that I remember are still there. I pray that you're happy.
Even if it's not with me.

The Fragments Belong Together

Things just break sometimes. Maybe we should blame that third person we became, that personality we shared together. Maybe it's their fault because you're a good person and I think I'm a good person too. We just weren't made for this.

The Signal Fire

You can never lose yourself so much that I won't find you.
And remind you of what it felt like to be here.

The Sheer Arrogance Of Loneliness

Making love was never about you and me in a bed. We made love whenever we held hands.

The Phantom Limbs

And when we speak now, seldom as that is, the old language returns. I
wonder if it makes old names make guest appearances in your mind. If
you can feel the skin of my neck near yours one more time. Do you
reach across the bed for a shape, no longer there. Do you remember
it clearly or is it all just memories of memories. Is there still warmth
from my fingers tracing the contours of your skin, left somewhere in
your body. If you smell the smell of how I used to smell in a crowd,
do you think of these things. Is something missing in everyone else's
or someone new's voice. Will they never know quite how to laugh
or breathe just behind your ear. Do they know what you look like
when you want to leave a party, when you've had too much of people.
Could they rebuild your body out of clay if they needed to, because
they've touched it so many times. Does your back still arch the way it
used to when I still kissed you.

Does an old singer sing an old song on an old radio.

Do the lyrics still shake your fucking soul.

Did it sound like this?

The Stars Whisper To Planes (Sometimes Trains)

Services were held for us at major international airports and the same
song was played each time, the one I'd play outside your bedroom
window each night if I could.

The Close And The Nearly

Something has moved and bumped the cradle of everything. The
world is out of sync. Birds fly backwards and the fish swim through the
air. Hours pass like seconds and seconds pass like hours. The light fades
before the sun leaves. The stars shine before the night falls. I am here
early. You are here late.

The Person Happiness Became

So if you love me but you don't need me, you don't love me.

❧

The Union Of Steel And Space

I write the love letters you never got, the ones you never sent. And I'll throw these words out there like confetti at the wedding you and I never had.

❧

The Translation Service

And when I asked you how you'd been I meant I missed you more than I've ever missed anything before.

❧

The Billions Of Pieces

The human heart is made from the only substance in the universe that can become stronger, after it's been broken.

❧

The Lying Tree

The least you could do, is uncross your heart. Unhope to die.

The Bridge From Solitude

Just like you mistook lust for love, you have mistaken being alone with loneliness. So I'm fine. Thank you for asking.

The Things I Meant

A heart was meant to beat. And air was meant to be breathed, close to your ear. And your skin was meant to remember what mine felt like. And some songs were meant to play on repeat. And the sun was meant to come down. And we were meant to ignore it when it woke up. And days were meant to pass. And nights were meant to follow. And your eyes were meant to cry out whatever pain was left.

And I never meant to hurt you.

But I guess that's what everyone says.

The Seconds Before The Launch

This isn't me missing you. This is me missing the me I used to be.

This isn't me.

The Voice In The Machine

Thank you for calling/standing near me/being concerned. But I am not here right now. I am somewhere else. And you cannot reach me. Please leave me at the sound of the beep.

The City Rises And Falls

You were a dream. Then a reality. Now a memory.

The Distance To You

You told me it'd be ok. But you were the one crying.

You told me to let go. But you were the one holding onto my shirt.

The Tree In A Forest

And if you're alone, I hope you know that I'm alone too.
So I believe we will be friends.

PS.

You are beautiful and loved by the universe that made you, with every atom and star moving in perfect alignment to make you, you.

The View From The Hospital

If you can't let go, you can't put your heart back in your chest.

The Snow Falls On Forever (Hush)

You can't miss forever.

No matter how close forever feels right now.

You can't hurt forever.

Even if your heart whispers in your ear and tries to convince you otherwise.

You can't bleed forever.

Sooner or later, you will either die or live.

Neither of us can do anything for forever.

Because forever passed away, long ago.

The Darkest Lie

I have cut off larger parts of myself than you before.

The Heart's Failed Disguise

This. This is what happens when you talk like a stranger to the person you once loved.

The Movements Of The Dead

And we lay dying, and we took turns reaching out to each other, just to check if either of us had changed our minds, to see if one of us still wanted to live, to give the other one hope. And you killed me a little more and I did the same to you, each time we did. Breaking the thing we were trying to fix. Trying not to hurt each other as we killed each other. Until we were both quiet.

Until the last remaining light, left us forever.

The Worn Out Shoes

I once left home and never stopped walking.

I once swallowed every lie I ever told, all at once.

I once hurt myself so badly, I died every day for years.

All because I once spent my time with you.

The Things I Have Done In Spite Of Mechanical Failure

We flew here in a plane that could not fly, across an ocean that would not let us pass.

To live a life we could not live.

To kiss the kisses we could not kiss.

And now our bodies rest at the bottom of that ocean.

And now all that's left of you and I, are these words I could not write.

The Last Moments

I think you reach out in the end, to feel the edge that ends everything, your blood still wet on the blade and some part of you, in those last moments, still tries to love the thing that kills you.

The Green Curtain

How many hearts would be invaded for the wrong reasons, if each time you said "I love you", you meant it?

The Midnight That Lasted Forever

I do not have to look at the clock to know that it's midnight. I can feel the day rushing across the world, as fast as time.

But somewhere, there is a beach that time cannot reach. Where everyone and everything has always been and never was. And perhaps, you are there waiting for me.

In that place, time cannot touch.

The Longest Shadow

You know what I would do for love. But no one ever asked me how far I would go, for loss.

The Missing Bread Crumbs

Stop telling me to follow my heart. It once led me to you.

The Expanding Distance Between Two Points

Making you regret what you did to me is not 'me winning'.

It's everyone still losing.

The Last Meal Request

You don't get to yell at me for being dead, if you're the one that killed me.

The Time Served

This one is about how music gets ruined by the people you're no longer with.

This one counts seconds between moments.

This one desperately dresses wounds with logical statements.

This one only makes sense to the person who says it, until someone else, understands.

This one is here just to fill all the space that's left.

This is one you hear every day.

This one is six words long.

This one, hates the last one.

This, is the sentence you still haunt.

The Garbage I Became

Now the TV's on at 3am and you're sleeping on the couch,
because you can.

Now the plate is where you left it,
no one else is going to move it for you.

Now the politics of blankets are gone.

Now the people on the radio sound so far away.

Now you've got no plans when you wake up, just keep on keeping on.

Now the morning fades to light, to twilight, to night.

Now you rinse and repeat.

Now you remove the sleeve and remove the film.

Now you remove the sleeve and pierce the film several times.

Now dinner takes exactly 2:30 minutes.

Now the earth hurtles through the universe around a giant ball of fire.

Now none of your acquaintances know they're really your only friends.

Now none of your friends know they're just acquaintances.

Now you've got to get used to being alone, like when you're born, like
when you die.

Now you're free.

Now you can do whatever you want.

You just have to do it alone.

The World Is Better Backwards

I never saw you again. You slammed the door as you came in. We yelled at each other about something that just shouldn't fucking matter but for some reason, it does. It happened. We spoke softly. We were in bed. I told you

"I love you."

You said the same. We went to movies and parties and friends and ate and drank and made love.

It all ended with my eyes meeting yours for the first time and the sudden, extreme feeling of expectation.

And now, how can I miss what has never existed.

The Glass Tower

Until you are no longer the pictures that chase me down a flight of screens each night. Until the part of me that you first touched, forgets.

The Laughter Stopped You From Crying

If you can pretend as hard as I'm pretending, this can be the first time we've ever met. Not the last.

The Forgotten Star

You keep telling me to be glad for what we had while we had it. That the brightest flame burns quickest.

Which means you saw us as a candle. And I saw us as the sun.

The Car In The River

This is the acceptance speech. The end of anger and denial. I accept that you and I will never be the same again. That while those days will live in my mind forever, they're over. I hate it. But I accept it. And I'm moving on now.

The Leftovers

I made myself from all the love you no longer wanted.

The Day You Shot Me In The Back Of The Head

The sun rose like it does on any other day, on the day you shot me in the back of the head.

I'd just made coffee and you'd come back from doing the groceries and I asked if you wanted some without turning my head to look at you, on the day you shot me in the back of the head.

And I hit the floor so slowly and so hard and without any real warning, on the day you shot me in the back of the head.

I knew we'd had our differences and our silences but I didn't expect it to end like this, on the day you shot me in the back of the head.

I thought there'd be more time, on the day you shot me in the back of the head.

If I was still alive at that point, I imagine I'd smell cordite and sulphur filling the room and hear the echoes bouncing off the walls, on the day you shot me in the back of the head.

I imagine there was a look of surprise on my face, on the day you shot me in the back of the head.

I wonder if you thought you were being merciful by waiting until I wasn't looking, on the day you shot me in the back of the head.

I probably stared off at a distant point, while you gathered your things together and left, on the day you shot me in the back of the head.

And I know that my body was there for a while and that the room was dark and that it was very quiet, because of what you'd done, on the day you shot me in the back of the head.

But what you might not know, is that I got up.

And washed my face.

And the sun rose again.

On the day after you shot me in the back of the head.

ON DESPAIR.

The Orderly Queue

Don't be shy. You can take another piece of me. Everyone else already has.

Until there's nothing left. Until I disappear.

The Ungodly

"You think you're God."

"No I don't. I know because if I was God, I would've stopped believing in myself a long time ago."

The Child With The Invisible Head

And what still shocks me, is how often the thing that hurts you, looks like the thing that helps you.

The Infinite Distance

Your poetry is lonely. And yet, you write to feel less alone.

The Dark Words You Walk Down At Night

This is why it hurts the way it hurts.

You have too many words in your head. There are too many ways to describe the way you feel. You will never have the luxury of a dull ache.

You must suffer through the intricacy of feeling too much.

The Centre Of The Universe

"How do you feel?"

"Cold and lonely. Since the beginning of time, everything's been moving away from me. That's what it means to be at the centre. I don't understand why anyone would want to be me."

The Sound That Ends The World

I'm only quiet because I'm worried that if you push me too far, one day I will open my mouth and I will scream so loudly, it will shatter and break the whole world.

The Audience Of One

You're too pretty to be weird and too weird to be pretty.
And you feel strange when people try to talk to you. So get a job, it's safer than art. Maybe people won't point and stare so much. Even if they're only in your head. Especially if they're only in your head.

The Bombs Destroy More Than Just Cities

If you want to make someone cry, make them think of every person who hurt them.

If you want to destroy someone, make them think of every person who they have hurt.

The List Of Changes

We can answer any question we have, like how do actors make themselves cry, so we never sit in wonder and wonder at the wonder of the world, anymore.

And anything we watch can be paused, so we never argue about what just happened while we were talking, anymore.

We cannot hope that we might have just missed their call, because our phones are always with us and if they didn't call, they didn't call.

No protests in the streets, just a button marked 'like'.

No one reads stories aloud, unless you are a child.

No letters. Just bills.

The Truth Behind Glass Mountains

This isn't torture.

Torture happens in small, dark rooms in countries with names you struggle to spell.

This is just mildly unpleasant.

This isn't heroism.

Heroism happens in churches that are also schools, performed by teachers with no names and no place to stay.

This is just a good deed for the day.

This isn't loss.

Loss happens on fields filled with poppies, in hospitals buzzing with flies, in distant deserts and late at night when there's no good reason for the phone to ring.

This is just longing.

This isn't important.

Important happens on bended knees and is breathed on last breaths with hands clutched tight, hearts tighter.

This is just a distraction.

The Heart We Share

Every time they cut you, I bleed.

The View On The Way Down

All the hardest, coldest people you meet were once as soft as water.

And that's the tragedy of living.

The Agony Of Being Other People

I keep wondering, how many people do you need to be, before you can become yourself.

The Ghost Farm

To you, it was just picking flowers. To them, it was a massacre.

The Covering Of The Ground

The biggest scars are unseen and unremembered, always from a smile you forgot long ago. We would never get anything done otherwise.

The Possibility Of Clouds And Thunder Showers

Oh, how I wish you wouldn't worry so. There's hope in every breath.
But when fear infects the bones, I'm told, the heart is always next.

The Princess Is In Another Castle

You cannot go back in time, even if you wish it with every fibre of
your being, your heart and soul, even if you think about it every day.
Trust me. I know.

The Reason The Willow Weeps

It weeps for you late at night, when sleep does not come easily. It
weeps for the one you miss. It weeps for the dreams on the tips of your
fingers. It weeps for appointments missed and it weeps for the tears
in your pillow. It weeps for the silence and it weeps for the noise. It
weeps for formal letters where once, language was spoken as close to
your ear as possible. It weeps for betrayal, intended or not. It weeps
for the friends you once were. It weeps for the colours faded. It weeps
for sunrise. It weeps for a death in the family and it weeps when a
baby is born. It weeps for the last time you touched. It weeps for
words that can never be taken back. It weeps so hard and so much and
so often. So you don't have to. So you can carry on. It weeps for you.
When you have run out of weeping.

The Joys Of Agoraphobia

This place is in my head and no matter where I run, it's always here, all around me. It's a big room and my voice echoes when I yell, and there are days when I think you couldn't make it to the other side if you tried.

The Hardest You Could Be

And you will find no fear here, in unkind words or the hardness of others.

And you will find no sadness here, in the meanness of the world, in the anger that comes from those who feel small.

And you will find no hurt here, in a million insults or a single, softly spoken lie.

Because only a hard heart shatters.

Only a hard heart, breaks.

The Name Of The Sickness

You had the sadness and too much of it. There's no chemo for that except time.

The Crowded Life

You can have the entire world around you and yet still be completely alone.

The Bully

No one would ever think such mean thoughts about you. No one would ever say something so hurtful.
No one would ever hit you so hard.

Except yourself.

You are always the meanest person you know.
And only you can stop you.

The Stretching

The world weeps for itself on days like this and you stretch and stare to find the things that make it worthwhile. At least it's not boring. You keep telling yourself that. Perspective is nine tenths of everything.

The World Woke Up

Please don't open your eyes.

The world is wrong today.

I don't want you to see it.

Those dreams of burning cars, of bankers crying in the streets, of the earth shaking, they're not dreams.

Just stay warm for now.

Just for a little while now.

Before it hits.

Before it takes.

The Way Glass Breaks

This is the song I only sing when you're sleeping. These are the words I say when you can't hear me. This is the way I look when you can't see me. And you will never know.

The Cosmic Joke

And yet, of all these things, we feel sadness the most. We are never buoyed upon an ocean of apathy. We are never crushed by complacency. We are never moved by the okayness of the world.

Sadness and pain, to help us flee danger and hurt. To help us get away when we're bleeding. You have a body and it screams "Something stirs like broken glass in my chest, leave this place, before I die."

An animal part of us, still here after all these years, breaks our hearts.

The Ornate Cage

You see suns that never were and stare at skies that don't exist. You listen to songs that were never played and read books that were never written. And your mind is so beautiful and full. But I'm glad it's not mine.

The Sheer Lack Of Existence

I'm made of dreams and memories.

I am made of misheard whispers in the dark.

I am made of glances across crowded rooms.

Of the closeness of strangers in a line outside a movie.

I am made of the corners of your mouth.

I am made of awkward elevator rides and the lack of security one finds on a doorstep, at the end of the evening, when one has enjoyed the company of another.

I am made of the train tracks that take me home.

I am made of ghost notes, from songs you never heard.

So forgive my absence. But I was never really here to begin with, anyway.

The Universe Is Arrogant

You know that feeling you get when everything goes perfectly, constantly and nothing's ever wrong with anyone or anything?

Me neither.

The Superhero Struggling Up Stairs

Dear Diary,

Today I let the mask slip just a little and all the villains come flooding in.

While I don't expect you, as a book filled with lines, to understand my predicament, understand that I will be home late tonight. There will be blood on my costume.

And the dishes will have to wait.

The Remaining Mirrors

And I hide because there's more to me than what you see and I'm not sure you'd like the rest. I know that sometimes, I don't like the rest.

The Ghost Of Too Much

There's not enough soil in the earth for how deep I want to be buried.
There's not enough water in the oceans for how slowly I want to sink.
There's not enough fire in the sun for how brightly I want to burn.
There aren't enough words in my head to say all the things I can't.
There's not enough blood in my body for all I need to bleed.
There aren't enough couches in the world for how long I want to sleep.
There's not enough life in me, for all I want to live.
All I've had enough of, is you.

The Medicine Is The Sickness

If there's one thing I hate, it's people who won't let me in on the freeway.

If there's one thing I hate, it's having to let people in on the freeway.

If there's one thing I hate, it's waking up to 50 assholes pretending to be me.

If there's one thing I hate, it's waking up feeling like an asshole because I yelled at those assholes.

If there's one thing I hate, it's people who turn the things I say into insipid greeting card messages.

If there's one thing I hate, it's turning a bunch of ideas into a laundry list.

If there's one thing I hate, it's that feeling you get when you scratch something new.

If there's one thing I hate, it's not knowing what's wrong with someone and all you want to do is make them feel better.

If there's one thing I hate, it's knowing that my mind naturally gravitates towards the negative and not being able to stop it.

If there's one thing I hate, it's people who become your friend, to become your friends' friend.

If there's one thing I hate, it's being really busy and using that as an excuse to ignore your email.

If there's one thing I hate, it's having to acknowledge that my feelings are my own, no one else's. And, my responsibility.

If there's one thing I hate, it's forgetting that and taking the way I feel out on the world.

If there's one thing I hate, it's people who criticise things, who can't take criticism.

If there's one thing I hate, it's going to the same job day-after-day for the same pay.

If there's one thing I hate, it's not having a job.

If there's one thing I hate, it's not you.

It's me.

The Nature Of My Body

That sound you hear, that's the sound of someone realising that sometimes, it's easier to change the world than it is your own life.

The Fire In Smoke

What I meant to say was, sometimes I stare at the cigarette in my hand and beg it to stop wasting my time and just kill me. But I figured you didn't want to hear that.

The World Leaning On Your Shoulder

You know all their stories but none of their stories know you.

And you've felt all their pain but their pain has never bothered feeling you.

So you take their medicine. Even though you've had too much medicine.

The Molten Core

This world is hard. It has sharp edges and points that cut. It'll make you choose between love, money and sleep. Choose love each time and sleep when you can, money — only when you must.

Because this world is hard. And at times, it is too hard, for me.

The Bandages Are Made Of Shadows

You and I both know, the dark doesn't make the bruises disappear.
It just makes them harder to see.

The Handmade Collection

The problem with you is that all your scars have other people's names
on them. Even though each scar is handmade by you.

The Underlying Truth

If you really want to know, I just hope I die before I get boring.

The Factory Defect

If we really are all connected, I'm sorry for bringing you and everyone
else down.

The Unweaving Of Me

At some point, you will have done all you can do and then, all that will be left, will be the things that leave you undone.

The Reason For Airports

You can only hurt someone until there's nothing left to hurt.

The Nerve Endings Shatter Like Glass

It doesn't hurt because if you keep hurting the same part of you again and again and again, the nerve endings all die. And when that happens, that part of you goes numb. That's why it doesn't hurt. Don't be proud of it.

The Act Of Living Is Lethal

You forget that even the strongest person to ever live had a weakest day of their life.

The Occasional Silence

You can walk into a room and spot them. They seem fine when you talk to them but every now and again, across the room, you catch them looking off into the distance at an invisible point that maybe, they once reached. They laugh a little different. They hesitate a little more. Now they know what it feels like. And something about their eyes when they listen to music says

"Turn it up until my ears bleed. Let it be the last thing I hear."

On hope.

The Winter Child

In bright white snow, when everything sleeps.

And hope has left you lonely.

When all you ever remember about summer is how it ended.

I send hope back to you, wherever you are.

I hope you remember all the people you still have time to be.

I hope the little things in your life inspire you to do big things with it.

I hope you remember that summer comes every year and that the sun, is still sweet.

I hope you learn to hope again.

I, still, hope.

The Protestors In The Park

And all around, people fall like leaves in the snow. But those who cut you down, do not know, they are planting a forest.

The Day We Stopped Dying

You're wrong.

The question is not

"How many times can your heart be broken?"

The question is

"How many times can it heal?"

The Sun Will Freeze Before I Do

I promised a lot.

But never that I wouldn't get back up after you knocked me down.

Never that my broken remains wouldn't catch fire.

Never that I wouldn't burn through the ice and snow one more time.

And you can slam your glaciers into to me, so slowly, and even though they hurt, I will not go numb from the cold, I will not pass out from the pain, I will look up at you and the world and whisper through bloody teeth

"More..."

The Peace I Won When I Stopped Fighting

I'm sorry, but no gun can frighten me and no word can hurt me. No wave can knock me over and no rain can slow me. No night can tire me and no fire can burn me.

Because I have found the strength to do the things I believe in, and the will to stop doing the things I don't believe in.

So I have discovered what it means, to be at peace.

And you, my friend, will never find a big enough gun.

The Trees Grow Quietly

The things you struggle with today are things you choose to struggle with.

Because you believe that what you want to accomplish, is worth struggling for.

The Heart Cannot Be Discounted

If they put you back on the shelf, in exchange for someone else, don't worry.

Someone better's coming along.

The Ship Made Of Broken Parts Can Still Go Anywhere

You only fix the things you feel deserve to be fixed, as if you're a special kind of person who doesn't deserve to sort their own life out because of who they are. Like your brokenness is a symptom of being you.

"I can let that wait, I don't need to do this because I don't deserve to have it done. My life is always only ever incomplete."

And yet, no one deserves the full benefit of being you, more than you.

The Refracted Night

You forget that, in the dark, we must move closer together in order to see each other. You were never alone.

The Great Burning Of Supper

It sounds pretty but I disagree. I believe there are moments in your life when you have to dance like everyone is watching.

The Difference Between Paint And Blood

I know you think you define me.

But each brush stroke thinks it's important when it's on the canvas and each brush stroke thinks that it's the last and that the painting will be done when the brush leaves the canvas again.

But it isn't. You are just the shading. You are a dot. And I am the one holding the paintbrush.

The Place I'm In

You cannot kill me here. Bring your soldiers, your death, your disease, your collapsed economy because it doesn't matter, I have nothing left to lose and you cannot kill me here. Bring the tears of orphans and the wails of a mother's loss, bring your God damn air force and Jesus on a cross, bring your hate and bitterness and long working hours, bring your empty wallets and love long since gone but you cannot kill me here. Bring your sneers, your snide remarks and friendships never felt, your letters never sent, your kisses never kissed, cigarettes smoked to the bone and cancer killing fears but you cannot kill me here. For I may fall and I may fail but I will stand again each time and you will find no satisfaction. Because you cannot kill me here.

The Trees That Decided Not To Die

As I put down my pen, I know someone, somewhere is picking up theirs.

I know that someone, somewhere is playing a guitar for the first time.

I know that someone, somewhere is dipping a paintbrush and marking a field of white.

I know that someone, somewhere is singing a song that's never been sung.

Perhaps someone, somewhere will create something so beautiful and moving, it will change the world.

Perhaps that somewhere is here.

Perhaps that someone, is you.

The Moths Arrive In Black And White

The bad news is, people are crueler, meaner and more evil than you've ever imagined.

The good news is, people are kinder, gentler and more loving than you've ever dreamed.

The Story Can Neither Be Created Nor Destroyed

As you fall, remember that you are part of a beautiful story that did not start when you were born.

Remember that you are the universe exhaling, a breeze waiting to blow across a field of tall grass.

Remember, you are part of a beautiful story that did not start when you were born.

As your body cuts through the air, think of only the things that made you smile, the people that made you love, the ideas that made you strong.

Remember, those things will never happen again but they cannot unhappen.

Remember, you are part of a beautiful story that did not start when you were born.

Remember, what you felt can't ever be taken away.

Remember, you are part of a beautiful story that did not start when you were born.

And it will not end when you die.

Remember.

The Danger Of Dreaming

Shhh...

Danger isn't always loud and angry.

Red, fire engine, fire, clouds.

A fight doesn't always end when you've been knocked down.

Fight, punch, fruit juice, islands.

Sometimes, the world will try and convince you that dying is the most polite thing you could do.

Please, thank you, no I don't mind at all, go ahead.

Sometimes, they will make giving up feel just like going to sleep.

You've done enough, rest now, there's no need to carry on.

You are not in your bed. You are on the street. And you need to wake up and fight.

Now.

The Bubbles Are Your Friends

And though the waves might bring you down and though the currents might pull you under, the sky is always still right above you. And your friends will show you the way.

The Importance Of Correctly Numbering Things

There are more grains of sand in the soles of your shoes than you will be given winters to dream or summers to make those dreams real.

And there are more stars in the sky than there are grains of sand on Earth.

We live in a universe so big that a dying star, in the greater scheme of things, is as significant as spilled milk or an unkissed kiss. In an infinite amount of time, everything that can be forgotten, will be forgotten.

In infinity, spilled milk and dying stars matter the same.

And if you're just someone brushing your teeth late at night or you're a planet breathing your last breath as you disappear into a black hole, everything you do matters just the same. Every breath you take is as important or unimportant as the sun in the sky or the moon in the night.

Scratching your ear, is a kind of miracle, depending on how you look at it.

The Finite Curve

You will only be hurt a finite number of times during your life. You have an infinite number of ways to deal with it.

The World Would Be Easier

The world would be easier if the homeless were all just lazy and all they needed to do was just get a fucking job.

The world would be easier if evil were a real thing, instead of just confusion, misunderstanding, miscommunication and misplaced desire.

The world would be easier if you could just be happy for what you had, while you had it. If you could eat memories like flowers to keep your heart alive.

The world would be easier if comfort didn't rest on the backs of the broken, if your swimming pool was dug by soft hands that never worked a day in their life.

The world would be easier if we all just got rich and famous and we were all each other's #1 fan.

The world would be easier if it were an automatic.

The world would be easier.

But it isn't.

The world is hard because it requires real human effort to make it turn.

The world is hard because you may wake up today but not tomorrow. And yet no one will accept "fear of death and a futile existence" as a reasonable excuse to miss work.

The world is hard because you will have to fight for the things you love or worse, fight the things you love.

The world is hard because the things you love will kill you.

The world is hard because it was made that way by thousands upon thousands of hard men and no one wants to admit we have no idea why we're doing the things we're doing anymore.

The world is hard because it's hard to forgive and even harder to forget.

The world is hard and you should just give up, right now. Just lay down and die. Nothing will ever be easier.

But, you don't.

The World Needs More Lighthouses

You can join the millions talking in the dark. Or you can stand up and scream light, out into the night.

The Oroborus I Fell In Love With

Where you are, right here and now, this is how bad stories end. But it's also how the best stories, begin.

The Water Flows Uphill

The heart is a muscle like any other and the best exercise you can do for it is called picking yourself up off the floor.

The Lack Of Apologies

No matter how you stack me. No matter how you arrange me. No matter how you look at me. I am still here and I am still the same person made of the same things. I regret nothing.

The Corners Of Your Mouth

And you asked why people always expected you to smile in photographs. And I told you it was because they hoped that in the future, there would be something to smile about.

The Title Screen

Just pretend you're in a movie. Be as brave and as full of love as the main character. Because we all need to believe in movies, sometimes.

The Layers Unseen

There is magic even here, in gridlock, in loneliness, in too much work, in late nights gone on too long, in shopping trolleys with broken wheels, in boredom, in tax returns, the same magic that made a man write about a princess that slept until she was kissed, long golden hair draped over a balcony and fingers pricked with needles. There is magic even here, in potholes along back-country roads, in not having the right change (you pat your pockets), arriving late and missing the last train home, the same magic that caused a woman in France to think that God spoke to her, that made another sit down at the front of a bus and refuse to move, that lead a man to think that maybe the world wasn't flat and the moon could be walked upon by human feet. There is magic. Even here. In office cubicles.

The Sun Or The Moon

Things change the way you feel. And things change.

The Golden Locks Phenomena

You are not too old. You are not too young. You are not too poor.
You are not too sick. You are not any of the things that stop you from
doing what must be done. You are right here.
You, are just right.

The Return To Green

Oh shut up. Every time it rains, it stops raining. Every time you hurt,
you heal. After darkness, there is always light and you get reminded
of this every morning but still you choose to believe that the night will
last forever. Nothing lasts forever. Not the good or the bad. So you
might as well smile while you're here.

The Perfect Apathy

You remember and dwell on all the things you've lost and ignore all
the things you haven't. Because your scars are like stars. Yet the night
stays perfectly black.

The Carrying

Picture them in your mind. In that moment. Freeze it. See every detail.
Hear every sound. Smell every scent.

They will carry you through the pain.

The Things Hearts Are For

A heart is there to make you bleed. To pass the time. To help you sleep. A heart is there to touch and feel.

To mend.

And to heal.

The Beauty

If love and beauty were easy to find, they would not exist.

Chaos and sadness exist in order for you to find the love and beauty in them. So that love and beauty mean something.

It's meant to be hard.

The Way You Lie Here

Don't you dare tell me nothing matters. Everything matters. Every fucking drop of rain, every ray of sunlight, every wisp of cloud matters and they matter because I can see them and if I can see them then they can see me and I know that there's an entire world that cares out there, hiding behind a world that doesn't, afraid to show who it really is and with or without you, I will drag that world out of the dirt and the blood and the muck until we live in it. Until we all live in it.

The Thought Wall

Some thoughts will chase you from your childhood to the end of
the house and back again. They'll sit there, hanging in the cobwebs,
waiting to be thought back to life. Hiding in the walls. The smell of a
book. The way the light shines at a certain point in the day.

But there are other thoughts, new thoughts, that can take the place of
old thoughts.

Think them well and often.

The Day

You have been given a day. This day will be different. Because today
you can do all the things you've always been afraid to do. You can feel
the grass beneath your feet. See the sky overhead. The smell of fabric
softener. The taste of coffee made by someone else.

You can live.

Today.

The Radiance

Do not be afraid to cry. Your tears are warm drops of light that remind
you how to feel. Do not be afraid to laugh. That sound is the song of
a world that loves. Do not be afraid to care. It is by caring that you do
what must be done. Do not be afraid to stand out.

For, in your case, you have no choice in the matter. You will shine
brighter than a thousand suns.

Do not be afraid.

The Stone

Close your eyes. Breathe deeply. And live forever.

The Slow Hope

I hope you get what you want or you want something new. I hope you appreciate how you feel now when you start to feel differently. I hope you spend your time with someone you love, even if it's just you.

The Ground Will Give Way

The bad news is, your choices and intentions, some people and places, those nights spent awake and all you've done, can lead you to the bottom of the pit.

The good news is, this wouldn't be the first time someone's crawled, tooth and nail, out of hell.

The Next Stop

Only because it's still so raw and real. Soon I'll just be a series of images that sometimes flash through your mind, when you least expect it. And after that, only a few will stay. Then, one.
A memory of a memory.

The Seconds Can Be Days

This moth lives for just one day, and yet, you will never see it fall to the ground and curse the futility of its existence. Nor flowers weep when winter comes. Nor the moon sigh when dawn approaches. We are only ever given just so much. But it is always, all we need.

The Crowd

You think you're the only one who feels small. You think you're the only one who isn't sure what tomorrow might bring. You think you're the only one who's scared the world might eat them.

We suffer together and hold each other tight because when we touch each other, we know.

You are never alone. Ever.

The Haunting

Sometimes the night is dark and stormy. Sometimes the ghosts of what you had run their fingers down a spine.

And when that happens, you want to turn to the last page. Don't. You'll ruin the story.

The Chemicals In Your Brain

And maybe something's missing in your mind. Maybe you don't work the same way everyone else does. Maybe you're just different. That would be good news.

The Safe Place

You are in all our thoughts. And we will keep you there, safe and sound, until you feel better.

The Time Of Time

If winning is getting up one more time than you fall down. If strength is more than muscle. If time teaches us patience. And knowledge gives us grace.

Then we will go forward. Remembering the past. But never yearning for it.

There is so much more to look forward to.

The Fact That I'm Just Not Perfect

(The highways are filled with the dead inside.)

The highways are filled with people on their way to other people.

(Look at the way they're looking at you with glassy eyes.)

Look at how lonely they are and desperate for another human.

(The world needs to be burned down. Look at the news.)

The world is filled with beautiful people. Look at the news.

(Never apologise.)

I'm sorry.

(I am me.)

No.

You're not.

The Roar Of The World

And while it may feel like you're in a stadium, in front of a crowd screaming that you must die, there are voices in that crowd, if you listen closely, screaming for you to live.

The Peace And Riot

You need to tell the person in your head telling you what you are and are not capable of to shut the hell up.

The Defender Of The Forgotten

You are nobody's hero. And nobody needs you. Desperately.

The Best Way To Run Into Traffic

It does not count if you believe in yourself when it's easy to believe in yourself. It does not count if you believe the world can be a better place when the future looks bright. It does not count if you think you're going to make it when the finish line is right in front of you.

It counts when it's hard to believe in yourself, when it looks like the world's going to end and you've still got a long way to go.

That's when it counts. That's when it matters the most.

The Children Of Time

January has issues with her mother, February is always talking about things he wants to do while March does them, April eats sweets and May pays for them, June is the oldest but not the wisest and July always has an opinion on everything. August never stops trying do the right thing, even if he doesn't always know what that is. September once saw something so sad, she never stopped crying. October holds the lift for anyone, vice-presidents and street-sweepers alike (for his memory, not for theirs) and November makes fun of him for this. December is tired but always hopeful. He has never once stopped believing.

Monday's obviously a bastard, quite literally as dad can't remember what or who he was doing. Tuesday's temperamental but ok as long as you stay on her good side. Wednesday doesn't say much and Thursday sometimes hums just to break the silence. They're in love. Friday's always wasted and she and Saturday hold each other tightly until their delirium fades.

But Sunday, Sunday knows she's the end. But she closes her eyes, and she pretends with all the strength in her tiny heart that really, she's the dawn.

The Limited Edition Of Everything

But don't worry, somewhere, someone's doing something beautiful and no one knows.

Seriously, a no one, nowhere with nothing is dreaming the Sistine Chapel in 3D and there are unicorns involved and no one knows.

Still, sing that song you sing about what it's like to never work a day in your life and everything is beautiful because it looks great and hey, everyone knows.

Who needs another song about worrying about the rent, girls and the things they say or what it's like to feel alone.

Maybe, who knows.

The Wind Stops Screaming

No storm is so bad that you can't learn something from it. You can grow in a storm. You can thrive. Rain cleans the air.

The Middle Managers Will Be Forgotten

You taught and turned me into what I am with fire and steel and hurt and hate because that's what happened to you. But I will teach and turn with love and kindness. I will kill your spiral.

The Autumn In Their Eyes

You are not there. Somewhere in the future, suffering for something that hasn't happened yet. You are not there, in a place where all your worries manifest.

You are not there. Somewhere in the past, reliving your old mistakes and regrets. You are not there, in a place where memories resurrect.

You are here. Right here.

The Wedding

Sometimes the sun shines and it still rains. The weather changes all the time. You can too.

The Unfolding

I saw them kick you and beat you till you lay bleeding in the dirt. Broken and burnt, with tears in your eyes, you got up, opened your wings, and hugged the entire world.

The Long Hard Road

If nothing else, one day you can look someone straight in the eyes and say

"But I lived through it. And it made me who I am today."

The Fragments Of Hope

Dear Future You,

Hold on. Please.

Love,

Me.

Dear Current You,

I'm holding on. But it hurts.

Love,

Me.

Dear Past You,

I held on. Thank you.

Love,

Me.

The Sky Is Made Of Wishes

On other planets, they look up and wish upon you.

Because on other planets, you live on a star.

The Universe Will Take You

They might not like you at school.

And they might not like you at work.

And they might not like you in a park.

And they might not like you on the moon.

And they might not like you in summer.

When you say they remind you of winter.

But this universe, will always love you.

This universe, will take you.

The Last Boss

Out of ammo and out of lives and out of credits.

Though my damage is low, if you fall, I will stand over your body and begin to fight where you ended.

In the blood. In the mud.

Until they bring me down.

The Glass Attic Of My Mind

What would you like to tell yourself today, to make yourself feel ok?

The Celestial Companion

Still, courage, my friend.

Still, all is not lost and you are not yet done.

Still, there are fires to burn in the darkness and light to cast amongst the shadows.

Still, there are moments that must be taken, fighting and spitting to the ground.

Still, nothing has killed us yet.

Still, the sky smiles on the brave.

Still, have the strength to try and hold the sun in the palm of your hand, once more.

Still, ever burning.

Still, the most beautiful things come from beneath the ground.

Still, the light is cast from the darkest of places.

Still, we labour on under the cover of stars.

Still, we know the truth rides high in our chests.

Still, the world has yet to end, no matter how hard any of us try.

Still.

Until we are still.

The World In The Mirror

I am not afraid of you. There's nothing you can do to me that hasn't already been done before.

The Day You Read This

On this day, you read something that moved you and made you realise there were no more fears to fear. No tears to cry. No head to hang in shame. That every time you thought you'd offended someone, it was all just in your head and really, they love you with all their heart and nothing will ever change that. That everyone and everything lives on inside you. That that doesn't make any of it any less real.

That soft touches will change you and stay with you longer than hard ones.

That being alone means you're free. That old lovers miss you and new lovers want you and the one you're with is the one you're meant to be with. That the tingles running down your arms are angel feathers and they whisper in your ear, constantly, if you choose to hear them. That everything you want to happen, will happen, if you decide you want it enough. That every time you think a sad thought, you can think a happy one instead.

That you control that completely.

That the people who make you laugh are more beautiful than beautiful people. That you laugh more than you cry. That crying is good for you. That the people you hate wish you would stop and you do too.

That your friends are reflections of the best parts of you. That you are more than the sum total of the things you know and how you react to them. That dancing is sometimes more important than listening to the music.

That the most embarrassing, awkward moments of your life are only remembered by you and no one else. That no one judges you when you walk into a room and all they really want to know, is if you're judging them. That what you make and what you do with your time is more important than you'll ever fathom and should be treated as such. That the difference between a job and art is passion. That neither defines who you are. That talking to strangers is how you make friends.

That bad days end but a smile can go around the world. That life contradicts itself, constantly. That that's why it's worth living.

That the difference between pain and love is time. That love is only as real as you want it to be. That if you feel good, you look good but it doesn't always work the other way around.

That the sun will rise each day and it's up to you each day if you match it. That nothing matters up until this point. That what you decide now, in this moment, will change the future. Forever. That rain is beautiful.

And so are you.

The Memory Of Beauty

I hope things are beautiful. And if they're not, then I hope you remember this moment right now when they are. Because you've got to hold up each and every other moment to the moment when things are beautiful and say

"Look. I told you. Remember this."

The Magic Camera

I wish I could take a picture of you tomorrow, and show it to you today.

The Things I Would've Said

If you're strong enough to take that blade and draw it across your skin.

If you're strong enough to take those pills and swallow them when no one's home.

If you're strong enough to tie that rope and hang it from the ceiling fan.

If you're strong enough to jump off that bridge, my friend.

You are strong enough, to live.

The War Against The Sea

You say that only a fool believes that everyone has some good in their heart.

You say that only a fool makes music in their mind.

You say that only a fool loves hate back.

You say that only a fool leans against the wind.

You say that only a fool takes on a planet.

You say that only a fool holds out hope.

You say that only a fool tries to fly.

You say that only a fool fights the sea.

Very well.

I am that fool. And I will die fighting.

The Grasping Of Stars

They'll tell you that you're the ground. Remember that you hold up the sky.

ON LIVING.

The People We Could Be

Being gifted doesn't mean you've been given something.

It means, you have something to give.

The Importance Of Breaking Things And People

Just so you know, there are certain people who were put here to break you.

So you could learn how to pull yourself back together again.

The Train Hit Me And I Didn't Feel It

You shouldn't fall asleep on your heart. It'll go numb.

The Truth As It Currently Stands

You will not remember much from school.

School is designed to teach you how to respond and listen to authority figures in the event of an emergency. Like if there's a bomb in a mall or a fire in an office. It can, apparently, take you more than a decade to learn this. These are not the best days of your life. They are still ahead of you. You will fall in love and have your heart broken in many different, new and interesting ways in college or university (if you go) and you will actually learn things, as at this point, people will believe you have a good chance of obeying authority and surviving, in the event of an emergency. If, in your chosen career path, there are award shows that give out more than ten awards in one night or you have to pay someone to actually take the award home to put on your mantlepiece, then those awards are more than likely designed to make young people in their 20's work very late, for free, for other people. Those people will do their best to convince you that they have value. They don't. Only the things you do have real, lasting value, not the things you get for the things you do. You will, at some point, realise that no trophy loves you as much as you love it, that it cannot pay your bills (even if it increases your salary slightly) and that it won't hold your hand tightly as you say your last words on your deathbed. Only people who love you can do that. If you make art to feel better, make sure it eventually makes you feel better. If it doesn't, stop making it. You will love someone differently, as time passes. If you always expect to feel the same kind of love you felt when you first met someone, you will always be looking for new people to love. Love doesn't fade.

It just changes as it grows. It would be boring if it didn't. There is no truly "right" way of writing, painting, being or thinking, only things which have happened before. People who tell you differently are assholes, petrified of change, who should be violently ignored. No philosophy, mantra or piece of advice will hold true for every conceivable situation. "The early bird catches the worm" does not apply to minefields. Perfection only exists in poetry and movies, everyone fights occasionally and no sane person is ever completely sure of anything. Nothing is wrong with any of this. Wisdom does not come from age, wisdom comes from doing things. Be very, very careful of people who call themselves wise, artists, poets or gurus. If you eat well, exercise often and drink enough water, you have a good chance of living a long and happy life. The only time you can really be happy, is right now. There is no other moment that exists that is more important than this one. Do not sacrifice this moment in the hopes of a better one. It is easy to remember all these things when they are being said, it is much harder to remember them when you are stuck in traffic or lying in bed worrying about the next day. If you want to move people, simply tell them the truth.

Today, it is rarer than it's ever been.

(People will write things like this on posters (some of the words will be bigger than others) or speak them softly over music as art (pause for effect). The reason this happens is because as a society, we need to self-medicate against apathy and the slow, gradual death that can happen to anyone, should they confuse life with actually living.)

The Violent Peace

You kill death every day that you live.

And I do my best to murder hate whenever I have the chance to love.

The Words Are All In Languages I Do Not Speak

And yet, when you get here, you are not given instructions. No one tells you that heart A is meant to slot into heart B. There are no diagrams about how you are meant to live each day or directions on how to assemble some semblance of happiness. You are not even told what colours to paint your feelings or, given a purpose and a reason for your life.

You have to make all of it up. You have to make all of it, yourself.

The Breaking Of People

You can try being broken and you can try forgetting. All I know is I am no longer broken about the things I have forgotten.

The Grand Distraction

And every day, the world will drag you by the hand, yelling "This is important! And this is important! And this is important! You need to worry about this! And this! And this!"

And each day, it's up to you, to yank your hand back, put it on your heart and say "No. This is what's important."

The First Day On Earth

First, you need to relax. I know it's not as warm as it once was but you get used to the cold and warmth can be found in the people around you. Secondly, do not get used to crying to get things. Some people never grow out of it. Avoid them. Spend time around people who smile in the face of despair. Learn from them all you can. Everyone is a lesson. A story. A unique and wondrous perspective on the chaos that is human existence. The more people you talk to, the more you understand it. But never speak if you have the opportunity to listen. Especially if you want someone to like you. There's nothing you can say that'll endear someone to you as much as really and truly listening to them. You are on day one of a sometimes remarkable, sometimes terrible, sometimes beautiful, strange and always completely unknown journey. Be ok with this. Worrying about what happens next will ruin the surprise. You will meet strange people along the way, some good, some bad. This is a pattern that will more than likely repeat constantly as you grow up. Some things will be good, some things will be bad. Neither will ever last forever. Nothing will stay the same. Appreciate every moment of happiness and remember it when you despair. Hold them close. And when you are happy, remember the moments of despair and think to yourself, "I told you so." Never let someone else define you. You are your own creation and only you decide how you feel, who you are and what you want. This can be scary at first but it is liberating to truly and utterly embrace your own identity. People who hate you for not being like them are not worth hating back. Please, let go of hate whenever you can. Accept love whenever it is given and give it out freely.
It is the most powerful force on Earth.

Enjoy your stay.

The Turning Of The Sphere

"You need to spin the world again."

"Why bother? So what if a few more babies are born. So what if there's heartbreak, pain and pens and doughnuts and washing lines. Who cares if there's forgetfulness and a summer and wine and clouds with faces and shapes hidden in them. That's all that happens every time I spin the world. It's all just a bunch of things that happen. Why bother spinning the world again?"

"Because pens and babies are worth a little heartbreak and pain. Because everyone in the world deserves every chance they can get to find the things and experiences and people that make them happy. So give all of them another chance. Please, spin the world again."

The Place Everyone Worked

If you don't think I'm important, you're a no one, not a someone. Because everyone is important to someone.

The Limited Opportunity

There are only so many of us born at a time and we are thrown into the world to find each other, to find the other ones who don't think you're strange, who understand your jokes, your smile, the way you talk.

There are only so many of us born at a time and we only have so long to find each other before we die.

But we have to try.

The Trick Of It

If this is ever easy, then it no longer serves a purpose and you should stop.

If this ever makes you live differently to what you're saying, then stop. Just stop.

∾

The Place Sentences Go To Die

No one knows where the words come from and if someone tells you that they do, they're lying.

∾

The Past Keeps Going Away

After you're gone, people will forget your name, no matter how important it was, and your face, no matter how pretty it was, and what you said, no matter how clever any of it sounded.

The things you've done will crumble and fade and the places you once loved, will change and be given new names.

You are only here for one moment and it lasts exactly one lifetime.

∾

The Sweet Release

If you blur your eyes, the streetlights become hundreds of ghosts going home.

The Wall Of Days

You will never meet anyone who has done something great who waited for permission to do something great.

The Words On A Tombstone

Do practical things if you want your tombstone to read

"They were practical."

Do what makes sense if you think it should say

"Their life made sense."

Do what the world wants if you believe in the epitaph

"They did what the world wanted them to do."

But if you want it to read

"They lived every second they were given
and touched the sky every chance they had,
they burned and blazed in all the colours the eye can see
and left a hole shaped like them in the world
when they left."

Then do something else.

The Person You Meet At The End Is You

The universe curves, as does the Earth. And as hard as you try and run away from everything you are, you'll find yourself where you left yourself when you come home. Just tired.

Fix yourself before you try and outrun yourself.

The Few And The Fewer

You can make the world beautiful just by refusing to lie about it.

The End Of The Tunnel

If you can see the light at the end of the tunnel, make sure it's not the flames from the bridges you've burnt.

The Wood In The Trees

You constantly look for a sign and when it's given to you and you don't like the answer, you call it a coincidence. There are no coincidences.

The Flowers Of 3753 Cruithne

Truly great people were once called weird so that today, you aren't called anything.

The Hope Of Symmetry

So you look for patterns because that's what humans do to try and make sense of things. In hope of some divine order. And you look in movies and songs and the things that you read for symbols, points and swirls that match your own. But the only real pattern there is, is the one you make when you hold up a mirror. And reflect.

The Things That End

Mourn what you lost. Celebrate what you had.

All things come to an end. Just as all things come to a beginning.

The Need For Honesty After Midnight

Not the first one in the morning or the one on the TV, the well-meaning phone call on a Monday night one or some you find on the radio — The voice that whispers between your ears before you fall asleep, that's the one you pay attention to.

The Whether Weather

You think you're waiting for help. For someone to tell you what the right thing to do is. Even though, at the back of your mind, you already know what that is. So all you're really waiting for, is a time when you're forced to do it.

The Running Game

You can chase the shadows if you want to. But all you'll do, is make them longer.

The Catwalk In The Sky

And it may look to you like I'm just walking through your city with my head held high.

But in my head, I am not in your city.

The Acoustics

You turn on the radio and fall in love with the shape of someone's voice box. And then you hear the size of their heart. The width of their pain. And the length of their dreams.

The Sweetly Sleeping

Dream dreams. Big dreams. Little dreams. Dreams in which you fly, live, die. Dream of things you've never seen and things you see every day. Dream of the future, of what happened in the past and what's happening right now.

But, whatever you do, dream.

The Search

You will only ever find what you're looking for. If you want to find something new and beautiful, you need to start looking for something new and beautiful.

The Choice

Life can be a constant struggle, filled with hardship and obstacles. Or it can be a grand adventure filled with challenges and intrigue. Every second of every day, it's entirely up to you how you live it. It all ends the same way. How you feel when you get there is the only thing you have control over.

The Change

You will be a rock. You will be water. You will be both. Never be afraid to change how you feel and never forget how in control you really are.

The Burst

Live like nature. Explode slowly, day by day, from the centre outwards. You won't notice how brightly you burn or how big you've grown until you look back. And then you will be amazed.

The Ignored

You are constantly surrounded by incredible beauty wherever you go. Stop. And look around you.

The Drop

Trust those around you. We all share the same basic human condition. We all want. We all need. We all love. We all hurt. So trust them. Even when you're falling.
We all fall sometimes.

The Grass

You didn't walk up stairs when you were a child. You skipped them, two at a time. You didn't go around the garden. You went straight through. You didn't avoid walls and fences. You hopped over them.

Life is too short not to walk on the grass.

The Forward

Always have something to look forward to. Make something up right now. Something you want to do. Someplace you want to be. Someone you want to meet.

And look forward to it.

The Worth

All your work. All your play. None of it compares to one night spent next to the warm body of someone you love.

You need to learn this sooner rather than later.

❧

The 5:45 Home

And in you and in all of us, there is nothing more than the capacity to be a force for, or a force against. And to wonder, how many people wake up each morning and can't decide if they want to save the world, or destroy it.

❧

The Place I Found

This is where I write something for you. This is where I sit down and open a vein. This is where I miss you. This is where I try and find the feeling of prickled skin. This is where I push the headphones closer. This is where I tell you what I think. This is where I tell you what I know. This is where I tell you that it'll all be ok. This is where I talk to a stranger who isn't a stranger. This is where I keep my peace, hope, love and happiness. This is where the wind blows. This is the mulberry bush. And around and around we go.

The Moment My Skin Brushed Against Yours

But really, all we want, and I speak for the entire human race here, is contact. Someone to let us know that we aren't alone. That the world isn't a dream and you and I really are happening at the same time, even if it's not in the same place. That this is real. You're really there. I'm really here. We're real.

This is real.

⌖

The Time

Times will be tough like old leather and gravel roads occasionally. Times will be easy, like Sunday morning, every now and then. What you do during these times will define you as a person and a human being. Your humanity towards others, your will to make the world a better place for you and those around you and your identity as a citizen of the world. All these things count.

⌖

The Notch On A Belt

Similar to tricycles, summer, winter, autumn, spring, bruised knees, your first kiss and there is no Santa Claus, life is really just a series of things that happen. Sometimes to you.

The End Bit Is Animated

We help people when big things happen to them, when you see them getting hit by a car, when a brother or a sister or a father or a mother dies, we're there for them because we can see that death kills more than the person it takes. And yet, the people around us who die a little all the time, moment by moment, who require the least help, the smallest sacrifice, are the ones we ignore completely.

The Meaning We Give To Words

And I'm sorry if I haven't written to you in a while. It's just that life gets in the way of living. It's just that my fingers were stuck together. It's just that all the paper in the world caught fire.

You'll forgive me if I haven't written in a while. It's just that all the envelopes made love to dragonflies and now, we cannot bring them down. It's just that time stopped ticking. It's just that all the ink ran clear.

My apologies if I haven't written in a while. It's just that words ran out of letters (these are the last in the bag). It's just that language isn't perfect. It's just, me.

The Knot

You're all tangled up in other people. Their worries have become your worries. Their expectations of you have become the expectations you have for yourself. Their dreams are slowly turning into your nightmares.
You are not other people.

The Hello

The Hi-hello-how-are-you?'s. The I'm-fine-and-you?'s. The slight nod
of the head. The threads that bind you to everyone else. It's coded
language for a constant reassurance.

"I'm alive. You're alive too."

The Ghosts

The people you know. The people you knew. What you've learned.
Your memories. All these things, these ghosts come together to make
up nearly all of who and what you are. The last part is your soul.
Your spark.
That is beyond ghosts.

The Waves Are Still Going To Make It To Shore

Stop thinking about what they're thinking about you.

The Intrusion

You are well within your rights to stand up, interrupt everyone
around you and say "This is not who I am. This is not what I want.
I'm sorry, but you've mistaken me for somebody else."

The Morning Bell

"Did you see them? With all their feelings hanging out? With their emotions exposed?"

"I know, what a freak."

"What are you doing tonight?"

"Crying myself to sleep, wondering why I never truly feel loved. You?"

"Same."

The Now That Didn't Then

But really, everything happens all at once.

Every single moment that's passed and the moments still to come are all happening right now, in this moment. You are young. You are old. You laugh. You cry. You smile. You win. You lose. You don't care about either anymore. You love. You don't. You love again. You hurt. You heal.

All at once.

There's nothing and no one to miss because it's all still happening. They're still here.

And it'll all continue to happen, forever.

The First Act

You have this idea of what kind of movie your life is and you expect the characters you cast to behave a certain way. To read from the script.

But the best ones never do.

The Ratio Of Life To Living

Oh sure, some people give a little bit each day. But there are one or two special souls who, when you least expect it, give an entire life's worth all at once.

The General Consensus

Love who and what you love because you love them. Not because other people do. Or don't.

The Art Of Feeling

You feel this way today. You will feel different tomorrow. Cycles and waves. Repeating into eternity.

The Place Where You Get Off

Outside the station, she stands with her child on the side of the street, taking pictures of cars.

You think she's insane. Until, one day, you notice that she's taking pictures of the license plates of the cars her child gets into.

Because you look. But you do not see.

And she walks out the shop with bags full of cat food. You think she's some crazy cat lady until you find out, she has no cats.

Because you eat. But you do not taste.

It's been a while since their last album but he assures you, he's doing just fine these days, white flecks in his nostrils. Then he asks you if he can spend the night on your couch, even though it stinks.

Because you sniff. But you do not smell.

And they say "Just OK" when you ask them how school was. Then you wonder what they're hiding until you find their diary and the last entry reads "I wish you'd give me some privacy."

Because you listen. But you do not hear.

And they've got a bruise over their eye and you run the tips of your fingers over it and ask them how it happened. You believe them. Until it happens again.

Because you touch. But you do not feel.

And they walk past you every day, one million stories, each waiting to be told. Waiting for you to ask.

Because you live. But very few, love.

The Beside

Those above you, will one day be below you.

Those below you, will one day be above you.

That's why you always treat everyone, as those beside you.

The Constant Apology

I pass too close to you in a lift and you say "sorry" under your breath.

What are you sorry about? The potential for human contact?

The Rope

Untie yourself. Get rid of the knots. Forgive your father. Forgive your mother. Forgive your brothers. Forgive your sisters. Forgive your children. Forgive your lover. Forgive your teachers. Forgive your heroes. Forgive a late ride. Forgive cold food. Forgive working late. Forgive being 5 cents short. Forgive those who have wronged you. Forgive those who will wrong you.
The last knot is always the hardest. It's also the most important. Forgive yourself.

And then you are free.

The Remembering

Your life will be remembered. You will be reborn on the lips of story tellers. A whispering around a fire. A telling of a tale.

You will become legend. Then myth. Then simply an idea.

Ask yourself "What do I want to be remembered for? What idea do I want to become?"

Then answer yourself. And do it.

The Something

Learn four new things every day. Something about yourself. Something about the people you love. Something about the world. And something about a stranger.

The Tracks Go On Forever

I never sat down and decided to become a story.

I just wanted to tell one.

I never wanted to be thought of as special.

Just human.

I never set out to help people or make them feel better.

I just needed you because I felt alone.

I never wanted any credit for the way you feel.

I just want you to know.

The Child

The most important thing you can do right now, is picture yourself when you were five years old and give yourself a hug.

The Series

There are moments of such pure, sublime, unparalleled perfection that they will force you to close your eyes and hold on to them as best you can.

Life is a series of these moments. Everything else is just waiting for them.

The Sayings Mean Nothing

The people who told you that the early bird catches the worm are also the same people who'll tell you later, after you've eaten a worm, that only fools rush in where angels fear to tread.

The Time It Rained Underwater

But nothing is wasted. There's no song you can listen to, no person you can speak to, no moment it takes to see things as they are that doesn't teach you something.

You need everything you know.

The Practical Guide To Consumables

You should eat to fill your stomach, not your soul. And drink to numb
your thirst, not your pain.

The Plea

Please words. I need you now (the and and you two especially). I need
you to tell the truth. To say things as they are. Don't be words that
I say too fast, words that I have to defend. Please don't listen to me
when I tell you to do the wrong things, be the words you were meant
to be. Be honour and fireplace and cellar door. Be slow and sunrise and
sunset. Be a phrase "I know they come again." No words more than
needed, just enough to say what I mean and mean what I say. Please
words. Work.

The Chance For Light

No gods or devils. No angels or demons. No group of people
controlling the world. Not the greatest person to ever live. Not the
worst. Just people. Just a person. Just like you and me.

The Peace And The Star

You think bravery is to fight and courage is to die. But the bravest
ones stand in front of those who would and say

"We will not fight. Because courage is to live."

The Metronome Tree

Forget about your lists and do what you can because that's all you can do. Phone up the people you miss and tell them you love them. Hug those close to you as hard as you can. Because you are always only a drunk driver's stupidity, a nervous shopkeeper's mistake, a doctor's best attempts and an old age away from forever.

The Truth Will Be Turned Up

Items will say "no known compatible issues" because there will be no known compatible issues and there won't be any jails or courts or manuals or propriety or form signing and faxing because you will trust me and I will trust you.

The Foreign Holiday

If you've never felt your ribs pushing against your skin.

If you know when you're next going to eat.

If you slept under a roof last night.

If you know how to use a computer.

If you can read these words.

If you know someone you can share this with.

You have a lot to be thankful for.

The Day In The Life

You read the news today, oh boy.

22 dead and rising in xenophobic attacks in South Africa, thousands of refugees and a government in complete denial.

And yet somehow, all the people around you can talk about is where they're going on holiday.

They wouldn't laugh, if they'd seen the photograph.

❧

The Once, Twice

It only hurt the first time so you'd know how much it didn't hurt the second time.

❧

The Could

Why do you do what you do? Is it to impress those around you? Your family? Your friends? Your lover?

Do you do it to make money? To live in a nice house? To buy things that can't be scratched?

Or do you do it because you love it. Because it lets you finish each day with a smile on your face and a thought in your mind.

"Today I did the best I could do. Not because I had to. Because I wanted to."

The Suit

The mask covered your face. The artificial voice box warped what you were saying. The gloves covered your hands, hiding any last hint of colour. You told me that it obscured your race and any heritage it held. The sins of your father. The dreams of your mother. You told me if everyone wore one, then no one could judge anyone anymore.

I told you it looked terrible. You told me:

Exactly.

The Watching

Watching you. While you watch me. Watching back.

The Hard

You called me over when I was young and told me you wanted to see how strong I was. I was eager to impress you so I obliged. You told me to put my hand in front of my face and try to keep it there, while you tried to pull it away.
I thought I was doing so well as I strained against your arm. Until you let go. And I hit myself so hard I ended up on the ground with a bleeding nose.
You helped me up, after you'd finished laughing, and said "Let that be a lesson. Trust no one. Not even me."
Despite what had happened, there was more love in that sentence than a thousand bed time stories.

The Playing

Every time you win, someone else has to lose. Don't play to win. Play to play.

The Tired Ramblings

Okay so you're out the gates and in the race and you get an education and a job and a wife and a kid and you drink and you eat and you make love when you can sometimes more than you can and you consume things like your lover and a cigarette and a drink and a bite to eat before you go to sleep and then wake up and do it again because you can and you will and that's what's expected of you just like they expected it of your father and his father before him and one day they'll expect it from your kids too and then their kids will follow your over trodden footsteps into the office and get a cup of coffee and talk by the water cooler about what movies they saw last night.

You need to slow down. There is more than this.

The Wires

I never met you but I knew all your secrets. You'd spill them late at night across the wires, across the Earth, from one continent to another. I don't know what you sounded like but I knew what you'd say. And I didn't even know what you looked like. But I knew how you felt. We trust in strangers the most.

The Way Home

Take the long way home. It's harder but you'll be a better person for it.
Live interestingly.

The Final Exam

a) Rain is the sound of the night rolling over in its sleep.

b) Rain is a record of broken promises and each one is sent back to
Earth to clean it.

c) Rain is life by a 1000 cuts.

d) Rain is a coronary anesthetic.

e) Rain is the world secretly crying for you, when no one else will.

The Saviour Got Lost In The Mirror

If the only reason you help is so that you can tell people that you help,
I don't need your help.

The Forest Of Rain

Understand that, the prisons you've built are of your own design.

Understand that, you should be the person you wanted to be when you woke up this morning.

Understand that, the world desperately wants to love you, if you'll let it.

Understand that, you deserve that love, even if you don't feel like it.

Understand that, love can hit a planet like a comet.

Understand that, the rain can unrain, if you want it to.

The Wonderful Flaws You Could Have

Everyone edits themselves here, and it makes me wonder whether you're ever actually connected to real people, or just the people they all wish they were.

The Red Sky At Night

Today, no planes flew into any buildings.

Today, there was no fire falling from the sky.

Today, there were no riots in the streets.

Today, the news was mostly just about famous people.

Today, no shaky footage was recorded of children running from a burning village.

Today, not one person stood in front of a tank.

Today, no one put flowers in the rifle barrels of guns.

Today, you will check your mail.

Today, no shots rang out over a black cavalcade.

Today, there was no negotiated revolution.

Today, no flags were burned.

Today, sport will be played and people will be upset over the outcome.

Tomorrow however, is a new day.

The Board And The Dice

It's a simple game. You win when you stop caring about it.

❦

The Nod And The Wink

Time never said

"Best you enjoy yourself now because we're going somewhere soon."

But that's what he meant.

❦

The Shell Against Your Ear

Maybe we're notes, plucked from strings we cannot see. Maybe we're all echoes of each other. Maybe that sound is all you are.

❦

The Anthems For People (Not Places)

If life was a song, would you spend most of it worrying about how it ended?

If life was a song, would there be meaning in the sound?

If life was a song, would you, please, sing it with me?

The State Of The Artist

You, as an artist, have the greatest responsibility of all.

You are charged with trying to make people feel, in a world that tells them not to.

You are tasked with speaking soft words, painting, playing, filming, writing moments of such magnitude and beauty that people rediscover their hearts one more (last) time.

You are here to give meaning to the few decades we spend here.

That is the reason you were sent to Earth.

The Things I Have Felt Have Torn Me Apart

Those who walk away from you in the dark should be forgotten in the light.

The House We Keep Moments In

May you do the things you want to and always remember what it felt like when you were doing them.

The Black Ink In Their Eyes

The problem is you think poetry is about words. But the greatest poets I ever met, never wrote a single word.

The Fragile Alliances

Sometimes I can't work out if you're a friend who wants to talk to me or an enemy who wants to take from me.

                ⤴

The Messenger Was Dead When I Got Here

You should tell them the truth. Tell them that if they hold on too tightly, love might cut them. Tell them to hold on tightly anyway. Tell them everything is worth it and that the richness of life is only ever enhanced by its inevitable, brief flashes of sadness and loss.

                ⤴

The Upsidedowness Of Everything

So yes, I laughed. I laughed at the pain and the futility and the frustration and the heartache to keep it separate from me. And while it may seem like insanity to you, it is the thing that prevents it, for me.

The List Of Reasons

That the way light bounces off your skin has nothing to do with who you are.

That smokers believe they need to die a little, just to go outside.

That art has always hated the frame you put it in and would lash out, kicking and screaming in the streets, if you gave it half a chance.

That the way lovers touch cannot be communicated in words, no matter how often or how hard you try.

That your body fights your mind and your mind fights your soul and your soul fights the world, to try and figure out what you are.

That sometimes, you're just tired.

That's all.

The Points Of Light

You are more than a series of experiences. You are the light that surrounds them.

And if you're too busy to stop and actually look at what it's all adding up to, then that's what you should be busy with.

The Eventual Ghost

You have until the hour you die to do everything you've ever really wanted to do and say everything you've ever really wanted to say. It sounds less fair when you get older.

❧

The Pain Of Each Other

I do not understand why you would go out of your way to hurt each other, when life can already hurt so much.

❧

The Clearest Lens

And may you never wish that life would pass with background music in a black and white montage. And may you lust and hunger for every awkward second of real life, in all its un-retouched glory.

❧

The Forest Of The Sun

I picked up my hat and started to write.

"You are a place in a story, in which I stop and find myself.

You are my best problem.

And I want you to feel this. Because this is what it feels like."

The Experience Becomes A Story

The horror you face today will become the funny story you tell tomorrow.

In the end, everything is overcome and a life is lived.

The Defiance Of The Different

Most importantly, if you can at all avoid it, don't be normal. Strive, burn and do everything you can to avoid being the industry standard. Even the highest industry standard. Be greater than anything anyone else has ever dreamed of you. Don't settle for pats on the back, salary increases, a nod-and-a-smile. Instead, rage against the tepidness of the mundane with every fibre of whatever makes you, you. Change this place.

Please, do that for me.

The Efficiency And Perfection Of The Lost

Yet you still value the things you've lost the most. Because the things you've lost are still perfect in your head. They never rusted. They never broke. They are made of the memories you once had, which only grow rosier and brighter, day by day. They are made of the dreams of how wonderful things could have been and must never suffer the indignity of actually still existing. Of being real. Of having flaws. Of breaking and deteriorating.

Only the things you no longer have will always be perfect.

The World Needs More Fun (And Less Ice)

The only reason any of it exists, is so that you can have fun while you're here.

⌘

The Tragedy Of Self-Hate

The entire world is guilty whenever a person takes their own life. We owe it to each other to love each other, to keep each other around. This applies to you too.

⌘

The Assurance That It'll Be Different One Day

Don't you worry. Everything will be easier when they can just plug a fountain pen nib straight into your heart.

⌘

The Brightness Burning

You move closer to the person who is closest to the fire, because the idea of watching someone burn alive fascinates us.

⌘

The History Of The Planet

The nature of the world is such that at some point, my grandfather probably tried to kill yours. I'm glad he didn't. Because of you.

The Start Of The World Wide War

Please know that they shot first, when they tried to outlaw our entire culture and our way of being, when they threw us off our land.

Please understand that our only weapons were our eyes and our collective voices and when they marched on us, when they raised their clubs in rude salutes to the sun, we held up our camera phones and said over and over and over again:

The whole world is watching.
The whole world is watching.
The whole world is watching.

And when they were so ashamed of who they were, they wanted, needed us to close our eyes, they pepper-sprayed our faces, as we held each other close, as they revealed their true nature, to the tune of 1000, 1000 jackboots marching and we sat there and cried.

Please know that they did their best to divide us, to tell us that where the water met the dirt we were born on was somehow sacred, that the strips of colour on the flap of fabric waving above our heads were holy, that the way the light refracted off our skins defined our character.

They drove their cars through us in Tahir Square and they took our pensions on Wall Street and then they told us we were going to jail because we shared songs with each other.

I know that you do not have fat, bloated middlemen, I know the dictators have fallen, I know that the gatekeepers have all faded out and you live as earthlings, undivided by imaginary borders and differences.

Because I know I was born here on the blue electric fields, in the democracy of ideas, in the new country.

And this is a place worth dying for.

The Truth Is Born In Strange Places

Joan of Arc came back as a little girl in Japan, and her father told her to stop listening to her imaginary friends.

Elvis was born again in a small village in Sudan, he died hungry, age 9, never knowing what a guitar was.

Michelangelo was drafted into the military at age 18 in Korea, he painted his face black with shoe polish and learned to kill.

Jackson Pollock got told to stop making a mess, somewhere in Russia.

Hemingway, to this day, writes DVD instruction manuals somewhere in China. He's an old man on a factory line. You wouldn't recognise him.

Gandhi was born to a wealthy stockbroker in New York. He never forgave the world after his father threw himself from his office window, on the 21st floor.

And everyone, somewhere, is someone, if we only give them a chance.

The Fur

Be soft. Do not let the world make you hard. Do not let the pain make you hate. Do not let the bitterness steal your sweetness. Take pride that even though the rest of the world may disagree, you still believe it to be a beautiful place.

The Shop That Lets You Rent Happiness

"This is the one," the universe assures me from behind the counter.

"But I thought you said the last one was the one," I reply.

"No," says the universe. "I sold you that one so you would know that this, this is the one."

"Is there another one?" I ask the universe.

"I can't tell you," they reply. "It'd ruin the surprise."

The Whole World Is Watching

You're younger than you'll be tomorrow. You've never been closer to the day you die. Go. Now.

The Passport Photos

If you worry about how you look when you smile, you are doing it wrong.

The Packaging Of People

"But this is just another box."

"No it's not, it's the box we put you in if you say 'Don't put me in a box.'"

⁕

The Balance

Never love to be loved in return. You are playing a fool's game. The love you have is its own reward.

⁕

The Free

You make your own choices every day. Whether or not to get out of bed. To smoke. To drink. To drive. To walk. To have a job. To go to that job. To hate. To love. To live.
Sometimes you forget how in control you really are.

⁕

The Winter

I told you it was cold. You told me "Summer's mosquitoes are quickly forgotten in winter."

I only really get it now.

The Unexpected

Random acts of kindness are the only acts of kindness worth a damn. Surprise someone today. Surprise yourself. Constantly.

The Craft

Science and art. Washing dishes and adding numbers. Driving taxis and sailing ships. Find what you love. It doesn't matter what it is or how much money you'll make or what people will think of you. Just find it and hold on tightly.

The Envy Of Wishes

You wake up with a list of all the people you'd rather be. But you're already on everyone else's list.

The Angel Of Almost

Then I was somewhere else, and it was bright. A voice said

"If you'd carried on practicing that song you almost got right, you would've been great. Bigger than the Beatles."

It continued

"If you'd carried on working on that book you almost finished, it would've changed the lives of many, many people."

Then it said

"If you'd tried to reach the one you loved just a little bit more, when you almost had them, your life would've been completely different."

And I asked

"Is this what happens when I die?"

And the voice said

"Almost."

ON DYING.

The Gift Of Yourself

You would never guess but I have spent my whole life waiting for
someone who would give theirs for mine, never wondering if I was the
type of person, who would give mine for theirs.

...

The Day After The Crash

The sun still, surprisingly, came up and shone down onto the cold,
metal leftovers. No loud noises. No screams. No breaking glass. Just
silence and sunshine. You would be forgiven for thinking that this all
happened on another planet. It didn't.

...

The Sun Leaves The Earth

I am so selfish, so greedy and so spoiled.

How can I ask for one more day with you, when I've already had so
many?

...

The Rain Was Once A Cloud

Know someone as much as you can. Hold onto the moments that
define them. Then when their body leaves, they won't.

The Sky

Remember when we lay in the park the whole day staring at the clouds, telling each other what and who we saw? I felt so close to you then. Part of me knew what you had to do and where you had to go but in that moment, I'd have given anything to stop you.

I still stare at the sky at least once a day. Hoping that one day, I'll see you again.

...

The Last Days

I just need you to be able to tell people I was here, I felt, I lived and I loved as much as I could, while I could. And that the person that I loved, was you.

...

The Slipstream We're Caught In

If time takes me (and time will take me), I will come back as a single feather.

So please come back as a breeze.

...

The Theory Is Still Just Theory

And if I blink my eyes enough, maybe I will wake up and you will still be there sleeping next to me.

The Future Is The Past Waiting To Happen

And though you may not be able to imagine what I was like, I did live. More importantly, I loved.

$$\bullet \bullet \bullet$$

The Death Of Love

Oh love. Why is your body so still, why do your muscles sing no more, why does your chest not rise and fall.

Oh love. Why is your skin so cold, why do your eyes not trace my face, why do you not get up and accept my warm embrace.

Oh love. I have no regrets for our mistakes, no heart left to break, for you have taken it with you to the grave.

Oh love. Love that turned to death, death that turned to longing, longing that turned away from me, leaving me here to bear it alone.

Oh love. Oh love. Oh my love.

$$\bullet \bullet \bullet$$

The Gone

When they are gone, you will remember every single opportunity you had to speak with them. And didn't.

$$\bullet \bullet \bullet$$

The Missing Exclamation Marks

You're ok. Breathe. Just breathe. Open your eyes. Come back. It's ok. It's over now. You're ok. Wake up. Please wake up. Don't do this to me. Don't do this to me. Don't do this to me. I love you so fucking much. Come back.

The Birth Of Remembrance

I built you a house and a garden inside my head. I know you'll be happy there.

• • •

The Ghosts: Two

Buildings crumble. People die. Friends move away. But your memory of them will always stand. And they will be as real there, inside you, as they were when they were standing next to you.

Your memories are real. They are the dreams of the past. And they will live with you always.

• • •

The Dead Sunwheels

You'll be as shocked as I was to discover that their last words weren't

"Did everybody like me? Did I like the right music? Were enough people attracted to me? How did people feel about my decisions? You don't think I upset anyone do you?"

• • •

The Future Of Text Books

Should any child be reading this in a history book, you should know that we loved. I hope that hasn't changed.

The Priorities

It doesn't matter how much you spent. It doesn't matter how many people worked for you. It doesn't matter how far you traveled. It doesn't matter what kind of car you drove. It doesn't matter who knew your name. It matters how much you loved.

...

The Tears

Lots of people who'd never even met you were at your funeral. I was one of them. I started crying as we walked out, bitter tears that shook my entire body. My friend turned to me and said "Why are you crying? You didn't even know them."

I replied "That is why I am crying."

...

The Bargain

He gave me that night back and this time, I told you the truth. We talked and held each other till the sun came up. And as I went to hell, the devil asked me if it was worth it. I said yes. Yes it was.

...

The Here

You are already dead in my time. But you are still here. You are the whispering wind that sends goose bumps down my spine and the sensation of water as my foot breaks the surface. You are a lover's fingers on my cheek and a drunkard's elbow in a crowded bar. You are the grass beneath my toes and the sky above my head. So I smile. Because you are in that too.

The Time We Were

Do you remember when we were vampires? Do you remember when we ran through the streets at night, our heads back, laughing and screaming, so alive it felt like we owned the world?

Do you remember?

Do you remember me?

...

The Pressure To The Wounded

You know I just wouldn't be human if I didn't try and hold your hand as it disintegrated from the light of a thousand suns somewhere above Hiroshima. Or kiss the tears from your cheeks in Iraq, like the sweat from your brow in Zimbabwe. It isn't in me not to try and lift the rubble crushing you in Gaza or hide you in Rwanda. Like a last hug in a building in New York or the water we shared in Afghanistan. More than the blood we mixed in Flanders or the sandy beach we trod in Normandy. Longer than the fires burned in Dresden or Soweto.
I won't let go of your hand.

...

The World You Cannot Fly In

They've taken us from the edge of the sky (Where the sky is just our reflection, looking down) and brought us here, my love. I can no longer breathe and you, you and the world have begun to melt and fade.

They've taken us, my love, in their cruel nets and crude boats to their own dark sky.

They think us ugly. But we are not the ugly ones here.

The Day Time Waited For Me

And so, I wait because you have already left and my work here, is
done. I wait and wonder how my skin feels like it's made of love letters
written a hundred years too soon (too late). I wonder at the mystery
of life and how much of it can possibly remain. I wonder at pain and
hurt and love and time and how much of each I held. I wonder at how
I cannot remember anything in my life before I met you. I wonder
at the tiniest of touches and try, desperately, to keep their memories
alive. I wonder at loneliness. I wonder at how long it'll be, before I see
you again. I wait.

And I wonder.

...

The Stranger Died As I Walked Out The Door

Someone woke up today.

Someone woke up today and kissed someone they love on the forehead.

Someone woke up today and kissed someone they love on the forehead,
before they left.

Someone woke up today and kissed someone they love on the forehead,
before they left, they said

"I love you. Have a good day. I'll speak to you later."

Someone woke up today and kissed someone they love on the forehead,
before they left, they said

"I love you. Have a good day. I'll speak to you later. I love you. I
love you."

And they replied

"I love you."

And they kissed them goodbye.

For the very last time.

Someone woke up today. But they won't wake up tomorrow.

The Chest Cavity

"It just creates and then fulfills a series of needs."

"That's all it does?"

"Yip."

"So why is it so sensitive? It's not like it's conscious."

"It has a degree of choice but not nearly to the same extent as a certain other machine."

"How do you mean?"

"It creates lists."

"Lists?"

"Yes, lists. It orders the things it wants to do and then does them, in order of what it defines as most important to it."

"It doesn't sound terribly impressive."

"It is the most important machine here. In fact, it creates importance. It decides whether or not you consider the taste of something more important than the effect of it or whether the feeling of a song is more important than how tired your legs are. It decides whether or not it's more important to you to spend time with the ones you love than it is to be at work. It decides whether or not it's more important to you to pay your bills than do the things you'd rather be doing."

"Bloody hell."

"You know what the worst part is?"

"What?"

"This isn't the first time I've been called down here to fix it."

"It breaks often?"

"Not often. But it does break. I've seen ones that have broken too often or too much. Held together with bits of tape and string. A great sheet of nothing wrapped around, just so they can hold it together."

"Could that happen to this one?"

"It has the words 'Anything Can And Quite Often Does Happen.' inscribed across the front. What do you think?"

"I think it's insane."

"Correct."

The Light From Frozen Graves

"But I just want to stop feeling."

"As far as I can tell, there's only one way to stop feeling and that's to die."

"That seems a bit drastic."

"It is drastic. Perhaps the most drastic thing there is. There are other ways to kill feelings, like drinking a lot or working hard, constantly, pushing those around you as far away as possible until there's no way for you to reach out to them but ultimately, the only way to completely stop feeling, forever, is to die."

"I'm not sure I'm ready for that."

"Good. You'll be a better person for it."

"What do you mean?"

"I mean that the most interesting, amazing people I've ever met, the ones who influenced and shaped the universe itself, are the ones that felt too much but lived through it."

"That sounds hard."

"It is. It involves living."

...

The Camera Is A Bag For Memories

And when someone takes my picture and they tell me to smile, I still think of you.

The Correct And Proper Way To Feel

"Is this how I'm supposed to feel now?"

"I don't know, I'll check the manual."

"And?"

"It says that you're feeling the right way."

"What way is that?"

"It says that there is no right way to feel but, right now, after something like this happens, you do need to feel however you're feeling and that feeling this way, however you're feeling, is healthy."

"That doesn't sound very scientific."

"It has nothing to do with science."

"Does it say anything else?"

"It says you'll break something if you beat yourself up for the way you feel and that you won't be able to feel differently until you've finished feeling this feeling."

"Ok. How long will that take?"

"I don't know. How do you feel?"

The Headstones

Now that we can communicate with the dead, a few of them you might know, have something to say to you.

I know how you felt, even if sometimes you didn't show it. I know why now (I know everything now) and I understand. I wish I could've done more for you. I wish I could've known you better. My love for you is the one thing that will never die.

Stop being so SAD (lol). You're not the one who died!

Brush your teeth. Take your vitamins. I'm watching you.

...

The Crossing Of Soldiers

I have been on this battlefield many times before. I have seen corpses rise like flowers in spring to face the fate you bring, to battle the same battle, time and time again. I have seen them rip off their shrouds and put on ancient armour, just to be struck through the heart, once more. To find peace in the earth. To sleep. Until they are called upon again.

...

The Things Which Do Not Happen

"We'd love to let you in but first we're going to need to ask a few questions."

"Ok."

"Did you have the entire James Bond collection on Blu-Ray?"

"No, I don't think I even owned a Blu-Ray player."

"Ouch. That's going to hurt your chances."

The Arrivals Lounge

A plane landed and a man in a scruffy coat leaned forward and wondered if this was the one. People got off and walked into the large, gleaming white terminal, where they were either met by others (some in tears but everyone smiling) or if no one was there to greet them, they looked around, shrugged, sat down in one of the long rows of aluminum chairs and either listened to music or read a book or just stared off into the distance in the kind of shell shock that normally comes from long distance travel. Several made phone calls. One, for whatever strange reason, tried to go back through the gate, to get back on the plane. Security, gently, held him at bay.

The old man had seen it all before but he didn't mind waiting. He'd gotten quite good at it. There were exactly 128 chairs in terminal D. The roof had exactly 864 crisscrossing tiles. The planes landed every 11 hours, 59 minutes and 59 seconds. He knew. He'd had enough time to count. He read the paper. It was always the same paper, but each day, there was always a different story about someone he knew on the front page.

Exactly 11 hours, 59 minutes and 59 seconds later, he was too absorbed in the paper and the lullaby of the announcer coming over the terminal speakers to notice the small, diminutive female form standing next to him.

"Hello," she said.

He looked up from his paper.

"I think I know you."

"Yes, I think you do," he replied.

"You once swapped your last packet of cigarettes for a bicycle, in the middle of the war, then rode it for five hours to see me."

"I think that was me. I can't remember. I think we ran a grocery store together. I remember cobblestone streets and a newsagent next door. The children would buy comic books. There was a harbour."

"I think that happened."

There was a silence.

"How was your flight?" he finally asked.

"Good. There was some turbulence towards the end but other than that it was fine."

She rubbed her arms.

"Did you get everything done that you needed to do?"

"Quite a bit. Most of it I think."

"Well, that's all you can really ask for."

"I suppose so. The tea was nice."

"That's good then," he said with a smile.

"Are we supposed to get a taxi now?"

"No, not yet I don't think."

"Then what do we do?"

He cleared some space next to him on the aluminum chair then took his coat off and scrunched it up to make a pillow.

"I think we're meeting someone."

"Oh. Will we have to wait long?"

"No. Not in the greater scheme of things. They serve tea, just ask for one when the woman comes round with the tray."

"Is it good?"

"The best you've ever tasted."

By the time the next plane landed, she'd fallen asleep on his shoulder.

The Last Thing You Said

As you lay dying, we asked if there was anything else you wanted us to include in the book before we sent it back to you.

"Love, at every opportunity you are given to love. Be less afraid. Embrace each day (none are promised). Cry when you need to, it'll make you feel better. You were put on this planet to feel every feeling you could, do that. Everything works out in the end.

I promise."

• • •

The Second Coming

Actually, wait. I have more I need to tell you. Stay just a little bit longer.

EPILOGUE.

The Beating Of Fists Against Gravestones

Do not be sad that I am gone. I didn't go.

You are holding me. I am these words and these pages.

And I am holding you too.

This is forever.

(Never) The End

Other Books by Iain S. Thomas

I Wrote This For You is the first collection of the best photography and prose of the world-renowned blog, I Wrote This For You, from 2007 to 2011. Discover the blog at iwrotethisforyou.me

I Wrote This For You And Only You is the second collection from the *I Wrote This For You* project, it contains all the best photography and prose from 2011 to 2015.

I Wrote This For You: Just The Words was published in 2013 and contains 400 of the best poems from *I Wrote This For You* blog but only select photography.

Intentional Dissonance is a science fiction novel about Jon Salt, a young man in a dark dystopian future, addicted to a drug that causes sadness and unable to control his gift that turns his thoughts into reality.

25 Love Poems For The NSA was created in response to the information exposed by Edward Snowden, this short ebook contains 25 poems created using words that the NSA flags and tracks in email communication.

I Am Incomplete Without You is a collection of prompts and creative questions designed to inspire and provoke poetry in the reader, who then becomes the writer. Read excerpts and responses at iamincompletewithoutyou.com

How To Be Happy: Not A Self-Help Book. Seriously. is a collection of poetry, prose and short stories set within the story of the author's desperate attempt to write a self-help book about being happy.

CONTENTS

ON LOVE FOUND.

ON BEING IN LOVE.

ON LOVE LOST.

ON DESPAIR.

On hope.

ON LIVING.

ON DYING.

EPILOGUE.